A ROUND INDIANA

A ROUND INDIANA

Round Barns in the Hoosier State

John T. Hanou

Foreword by Maurice L. Williamson

Purdue University Press
West Lafayette, Indiana

97   96   95   94   93   5   4   3   2

The paper used in this book
meets the minimum requirements of
American National Standard for Information Sciences—
Permanence of Paper for Printed Library Materials,
ANSI Z39.48–1984.

Printed in the United States of America

Design by Anita Noble
Maps and charts by Joseph Mack

**Library of Congress
Cataloging-in-Publication Data**
Hanou, John T., 1951-
A round Indiana :
round barns in the Hoosier State / John T. Hanou :
foreword by Maurice L. Williamson
p.   cm.
Includes bibliographical references and index.
ISBN 1-55753-022-X (alk. paper).
—ISBN 1–55753–037–8 (pbk. : alk. paper)
1. Round barns—Indiana.   I. Title.
NA8230.H35   1993
728'.922'09772—dc20   91-46904
CIP

*T*o

Cheryl,
Erin,
Stephanie,
and
Amy

" *Generally speaking,*

our farms are utterly devoid of

anything like artistic features.

There being no indication of

original thought or beauty,

much less actual practical utility."

—BENTON STEELE

FATHER OF INDIANA'S ROUND BARNS

Contents

Foreword

Round barns are a phenomenon that appeared only briefly in the continuing story of rural America. Today they dot modern rural landscapes, survivors of a different agriculture and evidence of a time when agrarians were the rule rather than the exception. Not merely architectural oddities, they are, in truth, symbols of another generation's innovation and ingenuity. To understand this and thus their importance is to begin to understand the story of farming in America.

Before the appearance of the Europeans, the native Americans were the first agrarians, disturbing little of the landscape but considering it to be the source of provender, joy, and natural wonder that spiritually guided their behavior. The seventeenth century brought a new kind of human habitation to this land, one that knew little about harvesting the bounty of nature and saw it only as a rather unreliable source of food and fiber necessary for daily existence. However, as new immigrants by the thousands and then by the millions flooded this expanding nation, the era of living off the natural bounty of the land ended, and the soil became a resource to be cultivated and harvested. The American farmer came into being.

If such were possible, it would be thrilling to observe, in time-lapse photography, the change from the first rude farms of those new settlers in the early 1800s to the larger productive farms of a few decades later with their great farmhouses, their huge pin-frame barns teeming with improved livestock, and their verdant fields of corn, wheat, hay, and pasture. The industrial revolution brought these farmers tools to work the land productively and profitably. John Deere invented the steel moldboard plow in 1837. Cyrus McCormick presented his reaper in 1834. Barbed wire allowed farmers to fence the treeless prairies. Following the Civil War, the steam engine became a powerful source of motive and stationary power. In 1892, Froelich built the first successful gasoline traction engine. Within the next few decades, the United States Patent Office was literally inundated with applications for patents for grain separators; corn planters; wheat drills; horse-drawn tillage, planting, and harvesting implements; cook stoves; wagons; cream separators; and thousands of needed and unnecessary items designed to improve the lot of rural America. That truly was the Golden Age of American agriculture.

The dawn of the twentieth century saw rural America at the pinnacle of its glory. Better roads, increased services in the thousands of small villages, and then the addition of telephones and electricity in the 1930s through the Rural Electric Cooperatives moved the farm from a position of subsistence farming to commercial production. Fortunes were made and lost by those who embraced the new technology. Markets developed for the abundant produce. Rural society flourished. Churches, schools, business, and industry were established to support the half of the American population that tilled the soil. It was a robust time out there on the farm.

The present has not, however, dealt very kindly with the relics of those wonderful times. The traditional-sized farms are now too small. Great farmsteads now stand empty, moldering symbols of change. Small towns exist only as bedroom havens for people who work elsewhere. The institutions that once were necessary to rural life now have little to sustain them.

Not for a moment would I suggest that we abandon all the advancements that we have made. Such a thought would be heretical in the face of the obligations of the agricultural profession to the United States and to the world. On the other hand, to embrace the new and all its advantages, and dismiss, without a thought, the lives, the machines, and the institutions of the past that all contributed to the present is a tragic mistake. The remembrance of the people and their customs as well as the preservation of the machines, the farmsteads, and the communities is vital to our appreciation of the progress made through centuries of dedicated effort.

Round barns are a symbol of pride in the farm and the soil that sustains it. They are monuments to the reverence of the builders and to the profession of the owners. Precious few of these barns remain to remind us that we are not the first, nor the last, to love and respect the land. Those people and things that have gone before us are essential—all of them—to an understanding of the present. Round barns, and all that they stand for, must be remembered and preserved.

MAURICE L. WILLIAMSON

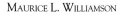

Preface

New Year's Day, 1985, was a typical winter day in Indiana—cold, wet, and overcast—but the roads were clear. Days like this are wonderful because of the solitude, and in my opinion, these days are the best times to take photographs. On this particular day, a photo excursion took me to Jackson County in southern Indiana. Heading over a small rise on a country road a beautiful white round barn came into view. I stopped, photographed it, and proceeded down the road. After one or two turns, another round barn as beautiful as the first came into view. As I photographed it, it occurred to me that these barns would make an interesting photographic subject. I decided at that moment to photograph all the round barns in Indiana. Little did I know that I would eventually turn up 226 circular barns and that this project would take eight years.

Locating all of Indiana's round barns proved to be a formidable task. Contacting the Indiana State Library in Indianapolis seemed to be a logical first step. Luckily, one of the staff in the Indiana Room directed me to a list describing the locations of 154 round barns. Compiled from 1968 to 1971 by the late Gene Worl of Hagerstown, Indiana, this list gave me an excellent base from which to work. During my free time, I visited each barn site, but I was dismayed at the number of barns that were no longer standing. Eventually, I discovered that of the 154 barns originally described by Worl, only a hundred or so were left—a loss of 40 percent over 16 years. It struck me that Indiana would lose a valuable part of its heritage forever unless someone documented these barns.

Up to now I had only been photographing the barns. With this new incentive, I initiated the Indiana Round Barn Survey in order to trace the history of each barn. I plotted the location of each barn on county maps and attempted to contact all current owners and relatives of the original owners. I contacted county historical societies and agricultural extension agents and wrote letters to the editors of Indiana newspapers. Response was mixed. Results were varied and often fruitless.

One of my major goals was to obtain a representative photograph of each barn. This was especially difficult for the barns that no longer existed. I contacted Gene Worl's wife, Evelyn, and one of his friends, Robert Peirce. Both helped me greatly by loaning out notes and photographs that Worl had collected over the years. Many of the photographs shown in this book's "Catalog of Round Barns" were Worl's.

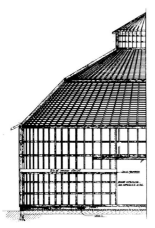

One of my leads put me in touch with George Gould, a retired Purdue University entomology professor and longtime round-barn and covered-bridge enthusiast. Gould's interest in round barns dates back to the 1950s, so he proved to be a valuable source of information. He generously lent me his notes, information about barn locations, photographs, and assistance. Later, I found out that he had collaborated with Worl in the late 1960s and that he had written an article on round barns that appeared in *Outdoor Indiana*, a magazine published by the Indiana Department of Natural Resources.[1]

As my research continued, I started adding barns to Worl's list. Gould added about ten, Bob Peirce added two, and three other round-barn enthusiasts—Eugene Sulecki of Rochester, New York; Larry Jost of St. Louis, Missouri; and Sarah De St. Jean of Greenbriar, Tennessee—added a few more. Many additional barns were found by asking current round-barn owners and relatives of original owners if they knew of any others. When asked, often they would recall, "There used to be a round barn located a few miles down the road," or "So and so used to have a round barn." Many provided me with valuable leads.

Published research on America's round barns is scarce; however, Wilson L. Wells's *Barns in the U.S.A.* and Lowell Soike's excellent book *Without Right Angles: The Round Barns of Iowa* were most helpful for me.[2] Wells's book provided me with some valuable historical information on about sixty round barns in Indiana. Soike's book is a comprehensive study on Iowa's round barns that I heartily

recommend for those wishing to learn more about the construction, builders, and history of these barns. *Without Right Angles* introduced me to Benton Steele, the prolific round-barn builder from Pendleton, Indiana, who came to dominate my study, and put me on the track of valuable old agricultural newspapers and photo sources.

After visiting all of the barn sites, researching many agricultural newspapers, and conducting many telephone interviews, I had compiled enough information to write a book. I purchased a computer and a word-processing program and started the long process of organizing and writing my manuscript. What follows are the fruits of my efforts, which I dedicate to the ingenuity of the Indiana farmer.

Acknowledgments

This book could not have been possible without the help of many people. Richard Embry and Mike Wood, both of Indianapolis, assisted me with some of the necessary map work and reproductions of historical material. I greatly appreciated the help and trust with old material given to me by Judy McGeath of the Indianapolis–Marion County Library, the staff of the Indiana Room in the Indiana State Library, and the staff of the Historic Landmarks Foundation of Indiana, all located in Indianapolis.

Deserving praise are those who provided me with photographs and unpublished material on the various barn builders in Indiana. I appreciate the cooperation of John Ridgway and Richard Ratcliff, both of Indiana, regarding information on Marion Ridgway and Nathan Pearson Henley. Special thanks to Shirley Koch and Linda J. Harsin, both of Kansas; Mary Hacker, of Indiana; and Lowell J. Soike on Benton Steele. Thanks to Mrs. Orville Detraz, of Florida, on Samuel "Frank" Detraz. I'm especially grateful to Mrs. Clifford Shively, Everett Gruber, and Peg Mayhill, all of Indiana, and H. Wayne Price and Keith Sculle, both of Illinois, on Horace Duncan. Thanks also to Dorthea Riley, of Missouri; Mrs. Walter Norris, of Virginia; Helen Barney and Peg Mayhill (again), both of Indiana, on Isaac and Emery McNamee. Deep gratitude to Mrs. "Hap" Kindig, Pat Zehr, and Shirley Willard, all of Indiana, on the Kindig builders of Fulton County; and thanks to Mrs. Donald Kingen and Eugene Pulliam, both of Indiana, on attorney Frank L. Littleton.

Sincere thanks are due to the staff at the Purdue University Press: to Margaret Hunt for getting this book started, to Carolyn McGrew for her tireless and scrupulous editing, and to Anita Noble for her excellent design.

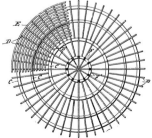

Finally, I appreciate the many responses to my survey and questionnaires from all of the Indiana historical societies, newspapers, and county extension agents.

A Round Indiana

*T*he beauty of Indiana's round barns has long been captured by photographers and other artists. To most people, the round barn is more memorable than its rectangular cousin—partly because of its rarity, but more especially because of its aesthetic appeal. The symmetry and simplicity of the round barn are perfect complements to the grace of the Indiana landscape.

Round barns are relatively rare in Indiana and midwestern farm architecture. Scarcely one-fifth of one percent of Indiana's farms ever had one. From 1985 to 1988, the Indiana Round Barn Survey identified 226 round barns in Indiana (see figure 1 for general locations). Because many barns have been lost to tornadoes, fire, or demolition years ago, it was impossible to locate all of them; however, it is not unreasonable to assume that perhaps as many as 250 to 300 may have stood in the state at one time. Of the 226 identified in

the survey, only 111 remained as of 1992. Nearly 40 percent of the surveyed barns had been lost since 1960.

With 226 identifiable structures, Indiana boasts more circular barns than any other state in the Union. Although nearly every state can claim one or two of these barns, most were constructed in the Midwest's Corn Belt. Studies by others indicate that at one time at least 215 existed in Wisconsin, 170 in Minnesota, 170 in Iowa, 155 in Illinois, 56 in Ohio, and at least 49 in Nebraska.[1]

▲ Rolled hay and a barren maple tree provide a picturesque setting for this true-circular barn in Jefferson County. Built circa 1911 and razed between 1989 and 1990, this 50-foot-diameter barn has horizontal wood siding and an east-west driveway through its center. Central driveways are found in 45 percent of Indiana's round barns, while horizontal siding is found on 25 percent of them. PHOTO: 1986

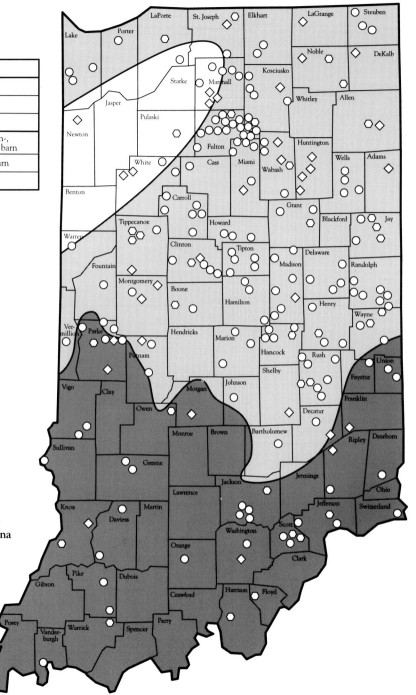

FIGURE 1
**Geographic Distribution
of Round Barns in Indiana**

A primary goal of the Indiana Round Barn Survey was to identify the construction dates of these barns. Consequently, relatively firm dates have been determined for 179 of the 226 barns. Construction on Indiana's circular barns began in the mid-1870s, with the majority constructed between 1900 and 1920 (see figures 2 and 3). The peak year was 1910, when at least 19 were built. Octagonal and nine-sided barns dominated the period prior to 1900, while true-circular and other polygonal barns flourished after 1900. Round barns built in other states also mirror these trends.[2]

Geographic Distribution

Indiana can be divided into three general geographic regions: a grasslands in the northwestern portion of the state, known as the Indiana Prairie;[3] a flatlands located in the central and northern part of the state; and the hill country of southern Indiana. Most of Indiana's round barns are located in the central flatlands (see figure 1), which was and still is the predominant region of corn, dairy, and livestock production in the state. There is a strong correlation between circular barns and the specific agricultural concerns of central Indiana.

The limited number of round barns in the other two geographic regions is due to specific characteristics of those regions. For instance, in 1900 the Indiana Prairie was a sparsely populated wetland generally known for its tall grasses.[4] The relative seclusion and scarcity of local timber may have inhibited the local farmer from taking a chance on building a circular structure that, in

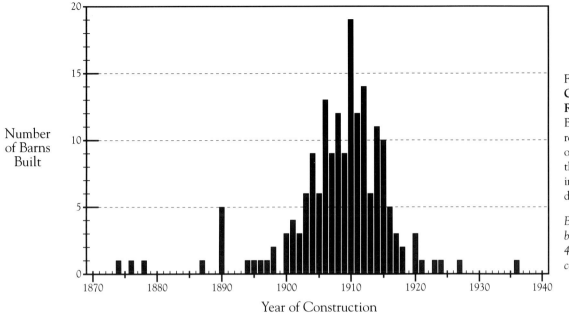

Number
of Barns
Built

Year of Construction

FIGURE 2
**Construction of
Round Barns in Indiana**
Business was increasing for
round-barn builders at the turn
of the century, but interest in
these odd structures peaked
in 1910 and had dropped off
dramatically by 1920.

*Barns not represented: 4 built
before 1900, 7 built before 1921,
4 built after 1940, and 32 whose
construction dates are unknown.*

some people's eyes, was not proven in its merit. Similarly, the hill country of southern Indiana has few round barns. These series of hills were formed by water runoff during the close of the last glacial epoch about 14,000 years ago. Like the Indiana Prairie, it was a secluded area, but travel was much more difficult because of rough terrain. This landscape limited the amount of tillable land and, therefore, was not conducive to large-scale farming. With less land to till, there were fewer farms and, of course, fewer barns.

Closer scrutiny of the locations of round barns reveals other distribution patterns. Throughout Indiana, there are numerous small clusters of these circular structures. Research indicates that the clusters are no coincidence; they are due to a number of builders and families who learned of the circular concept and convinced other nearby farmers to construct round barns.

By far the densest cluster is found in north-central Indiana in Fulton, Marshall, Miami, and Kosciusko counties. This cluster is of special interest because it represents what is believed to be one of the largest concentrations of round barns in the United States. Thirty sites have been identified within a fifteen-mile radius centered in eastern Fulton County. The majority of these are in Fulton County itself, where sixteen existed at one time. Fulton County still boasts more circular barns than any other county in Indiana and celebrates this distinction by having the Fulton County Round Barn Festival every summer. One family of builders, the Kindigs, is responsible for the construction of most of these barns (see pp. 30–31).

Other smaller clusters are clearly evident in Indiana. In southern Indiana, the John Hess barn[5] built in 1909 was the main impetus for the construction of at least four other round barns built in Jackson and Washington counties: the John Mahan barn (1909), the Howard and John Smith barn (1910), the George Stuckwish barn (1910), and the Elmer Williams barn (1914). About thirty miles east of this cluster, the Oliver Hardy family constructed two true-circular and two octagonal barns within three miles of each other in Scott County between 1916 and 1921.

Similarly, in north-central Indiana the John Leland family built three 12-sided barns on their farms in Marshall County between 1912 and 1914. In Clinton and Tipton counties, northwest of Indianapolis, Melvin Johnson and his brothers

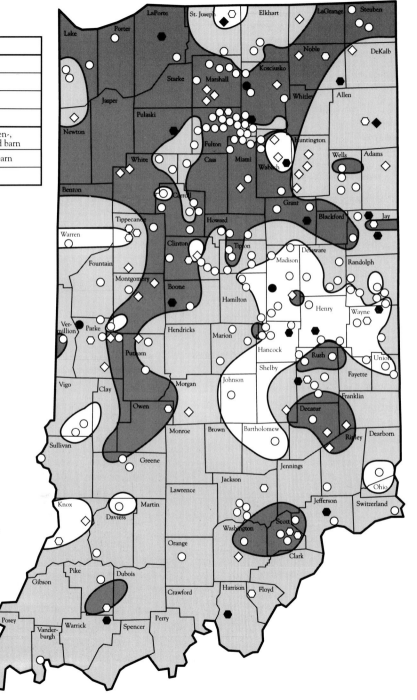

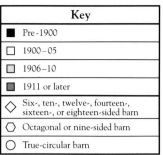

Key

■	Pre-1900
□	1900–05
▨	1906–10
▨	1911 or later
◇	Six-, ten-, twelve-, fourteen-, sixteen-, or eighteen-sided barn
⬡	Octagonal or nine-sided barn
○	True-circular barn

FIGURE 3
Age Distribution of Round Barns in Indiana

constructed three and possibly four round barns: the Allen "Duck" Spencer barn and the Zora A. Watson barn, both built in 1910; the Emmett Harper barn, built in 1914; and probably the Goff barn, built from 1910 to 1911. Finally, Nelson McCollum constructed several more in eastern Indiana in Randolph County. These are believed to be the two Frederick Retter barns (1905–06), the Howard Hormel barn (1908), and the H. E. Clevenger barn (ca. 1905).

Probably the most unusual cluster is in extreme northwestern Indiana in Lake County. There, in 1909, Edward Echterling hired Horace Duncan, a somewhat unscrupulous circular-barn builder from Knightstown, Indiana, to construct two 40-foot-diameter round barns next to each other and a round house a short distance away.

The First Round Barns

Where the idea for round barns originated is not well understood. Some writers have suggested that these barns have European roots, but no concrete evidence linking the two has yet been found. Some octagonal barns are known to have existed in France, but information and dates on their construction were not readily available to this author.[6] Other historians suggest the early circular barns owe their roots to the round churches, baptisteries, and mausoleums that were constructed in Europe in the early Christian and medieval periods.

Well-to-do farmers initiated the round-barn trend in the United States. Investing money in an

◄ The construction of
the John Hess round barn,
located on State Road 135 in
Jackson County, inspired
other farmers in the area to
build round barns of their own.
PHOTO: 1985

Ⅴ The two round barns and a round house built in
Lake County for Edward and Julius Echterling
represent one of several clusters of circular structures
in Indiana.   PHOTO: 1986

➤ The Shaker barn was large enough to allow a wagon to be driven in and out without having to turn around. The barn's central ventilating shaft helped support the roof and provided livestock with fresh air, which also kept the hay in the central hay mow from mildewing and rotting. ELEVATION AND FLOOR PLAN: FROM ERIC ARTHUR AND DUDLEY WITNEY, *THE BARN: A VANISHING LANDMARK IN NORTH AMERICA* (Courtesy McClelland & Stewart, Toronto)

𝖸 Some people believe that the Shakers, a strong religious sect, designed this barn after the round churches in Europe, which were built on the same principle of high central illuminated spaces and low aisles. PHOTO: 1990 (Courtesy Hancock Shaker Village, Pittsfield, Mass.)

Plan and section of the Shaker round barn

agricultural experiment such as the round barn added prestige to a farm and increased the owner's stature in the community. One such structure was a sixteen-sided barn designed and built in 1793 by George Washington. Constructed on his Dogue Run Farm in Fairfax County, Virginia, Washington's barn had a large central area that was used to thresh grain and hay with enough room left to house livestock. It is the earliest known circular structure used for agricultural purposes in the United States.[7]

After Washington's barn was built, numerous other round barns were constructed in the eastern United States during the early 1800s. The most famous was completed in 1826 at Hancock, Massachussetts. Known as the Shaker barn, it burned down in 1865 but was rebuilt later that year. Measuring 90 feet across with 30-inch stone walls, the barn stands as an amazing architectural monument to the Shakers. Inside is an immense hay mow 55 feet wide and 30 feet high. Stalls were planned so 54 cattle could be positioned around the barn's perimeter to facilitate feeding. The top of the barn has a large cupola with many windows to help illuminate the interior.[8] Shaker architecture and design is a superb combination of function and form, and the Shaker barn is no exception.

Another chapter in circular-barn construction was written during the mid-1850s when Orson Squire Fowler, a follower of phrenologist J. F. Gall[9] began crusading for the octagonal design "with a promise for a healthy and better life." This idea and others were presented in several of Fowler's books, including *A Home for All* in 1854. In his books, Fowler offered plans for octagonal houses but none for barns; however, he described the ideal barn as one with two stories and a ramp to the second floor. Lowell Soike of the Iowa State Historical Department wrote that Fowler "envisioned the ideal set of farm buildings to be an octagon house and an octagon barn. Nothing else would be needed."[10] Fowler's writings initiated the construction of numerous octagonal houses across the United States, particularly in New York, Fowler's native state.[11] Several octagonal houses are known to exist in Indiana, and Fowler is surely responsible for those constructed in the mid- to late 1800s. However, no octagonal barns have been directly attributed to Fowler's influence.

The first circular barns built in Indiana were indeed octagonal or nine-sided. However, tracing their construction to Fowler is difficult because both types were built twenty years after Fowler's promotion of the octagonal form.[12] And both types were constructed by farmers who apparently had little or no knowledge of Fowler or even of each other's type of barn. Both designs, however, served the same purpose: to shelter livestock and reduce the amount of labor involved in feeding and caring for the animals.

After the Civil War, a North Carolinian named Nathan Pearson Henley settled a tract of land southwest of New Castle, Indiana, in Henry County. There he met and married Abigail Stafford Cook, a widow, and soon after, in 1874, he started constructing Indiana's first octagonal barn,[13] an immense structure built with heavy timber. It had vertical wood siding and a self-supporting, sectional-cone slate roof, which supported a large

◄ Located in Wabash County, this pre-1890 barn is one of 33 octagonal barns built in Indiana. It was destroyed in 1990, leaving only 15 still standing. The barn's tall cupola, vertical wood siding, and self-supporting roof are characteristic of others built around that time.
PHOTO: 1986

octagonal cupola. Inside the upper level, there was a sizable hay mow that was used to store hay and grain. The lower level, arranged in a rectangular pattern, had stalls for livestock. To add space, a large rectangular attachment and a smaller one were added at a later date.

Henley probably obtained the idea for this unusual structure by reading the leading agricultural newspapers of the day, which were just starting to bring round barns to the attention of farmers. Undoubtedly, Henley was familiar with the work of Elliott Stewart, editor for the Buffalo, New York,

◄ Nathan Pearson Henley, builder of Indiana's first octagonal barn. PHOTO: CA. 1870, FROM FAMILY PHOTOGRAPHS COLLECTED BY RICHARD RATCLIFF, STEP-GREAT-GREAT-GRANDSON OF HENLEY

◄ From the late 1870s through the 1880s, Elliott W. Stewart promoted the octagonal barn in major agricultural newspapers of the time. His efforts resulted in numerous octagonal barns being built across the United States, including at least seven in Indiana by 1890. PHOTO: FROM *THE TOWN OF EVANS* [NEW YORK] *SESQUI-CENTENNIAL* BOOKLET, N.D.

V Henley's barn was destroyed in 1973, one hundred years after its construction. PHOTO: 1964, GEORGE GOULD

Live-Stock Journal. Stewart is credited with the initial design and promotion of the octagonal barn in the United States. In 1874, he constructed the first one on his farm near Lake View, New York, after his four smaller rectangular barns burned down. Stewart calculated that he could build a single octagonal barn to easily replace the former structures. Immediately after constructing the new barn, Stewart published the octagonal design and floor plan in the *Live-Stock Journal.*[14] Henley probably obtained the idea to build his own barn from this issue.

Henley's curiosity in the octagonal barn may have been piqued because of its uniqueness and the elevated local status that its construction could give him. However, the octagonal design also boasted several advantages over rectangular barns. In a never-ending search to improve productivity and increase efficiency, progressive farmers were always trying out new ideas. During this so-called "Octagon Era,"[15] mechanized farm machinery was virtually nonexistent, and labor was always in short

supply. Since most chores inside the barn were done by hand, Stewart's design provided the farmer with convenient shorter routes to carry feed to livestock—a feature that appealed to the farmer. It was also cheaper to build because it could be constructed with fewer materials and still contain more space than a rectangular barn. Another attractive feature was the barn's self-supporting roof; it was supported only by the outside walls of the barn, unlike its rectangular cousin's roof, which required interior support posts. The self-supporting roof allowed the farmer to fill the hay mow more easily. Finally, there was the belief that the circular form was more wind resistant than its rectangular counterpart and, consequently, would likely sustain less damage during strong windstorms.[16]

After the initial exposure of the octagonal barn in the *Live-Stock Journal,* Stewart went on to promote his design during the next fifteen years in other leading livestock journals, including the *Cultivator and Country Gentleman* of Albany, New

York, and the *American Agriculturalist* of New York City.[17] During this period, progressive farmers responded positively, making numerous inquiries about the new octagonal design. By 1884 Stewart noted with satisfaction that "some 30 or 40 [barns] have been built in various parts of the country—among them, five in Pennsylvania, three in Indiana, four or five in Illinois, two in Minnesota and several in Kentucky."[18] Henley's barn is one of the three Indiana barns mentioned by Stewart. The others are thought to be the Moyer octagonal barn that once stood north of Madison in Jefferson County in southern Indiana, an octagonal barn constructed in north-central Indiana in Wabash County's Lagro Township, or an octagonal barn that once stood in Floyd County in southern Indiana.[19] Of these, only Henley's is positively identified as one of Stewart's design.

After 1884, interest continued as several more octagonal barns similar to Stewart's design were built throughout Indiana. In total, twelve are known to have been built in the state between 1874 and 1900. Unfortunately, nearly all of these have been destroyed. Even the Henley barn is no longer standing—the victim of a winter's snow that collapsed its roof in 1973, one hundred years after it was built.[20]

About the same time as the first octagonal barns were built, a nine-sided variety was also developed. Unlike its octagonal sister, the nine-sided barn did not have the editorial support in America's agricultural newspapers, and there are no known advertisements or discussions of its advantages in similar journals. Consequently, only a couple of these structures were built. Indiana's best-known

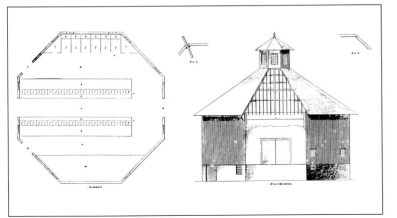

◁ Stewart's octagonal barn was designed to offer farmers convenience and cost savings, but its interior, arranged in a rectangular fashion, would later prove inferior to those arranged in a circular fashion because of the wasted space.
FLOOR PLAN: FROM *NATIONAL LIVE-STOCK JOURNAL,* MARCH 1878 ELEVATION: FROM *NATIONAL LIVE-STOCK JOURNAL,* FEB. 9, 1878

 The Door Prairie Barn in LaPorte County has nine sides, a peculiarity found in few circular barns in Indiana. It features eight horse stalls and one main entrance. Each stall has a window and a door to the outside. The barn's steeply pitched sectional-cone roof is topped with a tall cupola, another unusual feature. PHOTO: 1988

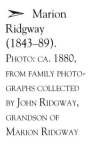
Marion Ridgway (1843–89). PHOTO: CA. 1880, FROM FAMILY PHOTOGRAPHS COLLECTED BY JOHN RIDGWAY, GRANDSON OF MARION RIDGWAY

A worker displays a horse from Ridgway's stock in front of the Door Prairie Barn. PHOTOS: CA. 1880, FROM FAMILY PHOTOGRAPHS COLLECTED BY JOHN RIDGWAY, GRANDSON OF MARION RIDGWAY

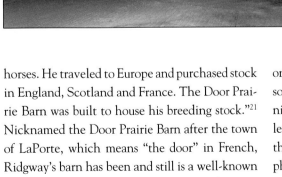

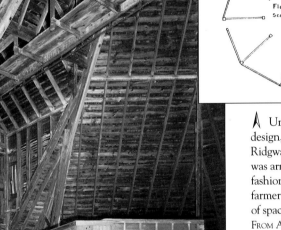

Unlike Elliott Stewart's design, the interior of Ridgway's nine-sided barn was arranged in a circular fashion, which gave the farmer the maximum use of space. FLOOR PLAN: FROM ALTMAN AND CLYMER, "A ROUND BARN," INDIANA FARMER, MAR. 1, 1902

An interior view of the Door Prairie Barn. PHOTO: CA. 1988, FROM JOHN MILLER DOCUMENTS OF MASSACHUSETTS (Courtesy Peter C. Kesling Foundation, LaPorte, Ind.)

nine-sided barn was built by Marion Ridgway in 1878 south of LaPorte in the extreme northern part of the state.

Ridgway was a serious horse breeder and successful businessman: "After the great Chicago fire of 1871, Marion Ridgway saw the growing need for better road (driving) and draft (working) horses. He traveled to Europe and purchased stock in England, Scotland and France. The Door Prairie Barn was built to house his breeding stock."[21] Nicknamed the Door Prairie Barn after the town of LaPorte, which means "the door" in French, Ridgway's barn has been and still is a well-known northern Indiana landmark thanks to its location on the main highway entering the city from the south. This convenient location allowed the ingenious Ridgway to advertise by painting in large letters across the sides of the barn his name and the horse breeds he was trying to sell. An old photo of the barn with the signs indicates Ridgway was well ahead of his time with the idea of outdoor

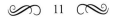

billboard advertising. Because of his endeavors, LaPorte became known as the place to purchase fine draft and carriage horses.[22]

Where Ridgway obtained the idea for a nine-sided barn is uncertain. His travels abroad suggest possible European roots; however, one author suggests the idea originated from Wisconsin.[23] Either way, Ridgway's design was very progressive for its day. It had a central feeding area—a feature lacking in octagonal structures—that became a prototype for future circular barns. Another special feature was that "the beams in the barn were all cut in a sawmill—not hand hewn except for the large sills which rest on fieldstones. Its stability is enhanced by the unique triangular bracing which resists twisting."[24]

Since Indiana's octagonal and nine-sided barns are dispersed randomly throughout the state, it is not likely that one designer or builder is responsible for their construction. However unusual the octagonal and nine-sided barns are in Indiana agricultural architecture, their construction represents an important part of Indiana's agricultural heritage. They were built by farmers who were progressive enough to try a new idea—one they believed would improve the efficiency of their farming operations. These early, experimental barns would set the stage for the design vigorously marketed as the "Ideal Circular Barn." A new idea was waiting for the men with the vision and energy—and also the ruthlessness—to turn round barns into big business.

The Ideal Circular Barn

"To Prof. King of the Wisconsin Experimental Station belongs the credit of introducing the cylindrical barn."

—BENTON STEELE, 1902

Popularization of the Round Barn, 1890–1910

During the late 1880s, when interest in octagonal barns was beginning to wane, Franklin H. King of the Agricultural Experiment Station at the University of Wisconsin was studying the merits of, and conducting the initial engineering research on, the circular silo. At that time, use of the silo for agricultural purposes was in its infancy. Researchers were only beginning to realize the silo's importance and the benefits it offered in farm planning and caring for livestock. Farmers valued the silo's capacity to store ample amounts of silage and other feedstock, which provided the farmer's livestock with consistent, planned rationing throughout the year.

➤ The research Franklin King (1848–1911) conducted on circular silos led him to design a true-circular barn that became the prototype for future round barns. PHOTO: CA. 1909, PHOTOGRAPHER UNKNOWN (Courtesy State Historical Society of Wisconsin)

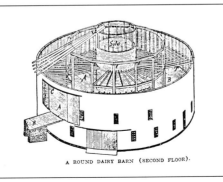

A ROUND DAIRY BARN (SECOND FLOOR).

⋀ This sketch of King's barn clearly shows the ground-level entrance as well as the ramp leading to the second-floor hay mow. DRAWING: FROM *PRACTICAL HINTS ABOUT BARN BUILDING* (Chicago: J. H. Sanders Publishing Co., 1893)

◄ In this cutout view of the interior of King's barn, the all-wood central silo and the sixteen posts that support the conical roof are readily visible. ELEVATION: FROM *SEVENTH ANNUAL REPORT* (MADISON, WIS.: UNIVERSITY OF WISCONSIN AGRICULTURAL EXPERIMENT STATION, 1890) (Courtesy University of Wisconsin—Madison Archives)

> The Henry Kemp barn in Madison County, shown here, was built circa 1898 following King's design, but unlike King's barn, which had a ramp to the second floor, this barn only had a lower-level entrance. The barn was dismantled in 1989. The other barn modeled after King's was Parke County's Robert F. Thompson barn built in 1895. PHOTO: 1986

⋀ This interior view of the Kemp barn shows the central all-wood silo and the sixteen roof support posts. The invention of the circular silo by King during the 1880s vastly improved farm productivity by providing the farmer with an excellent storage facility for silage, the main feed for livestock during the 1800s and early 1900s. PHOTO: 1986

Before the 1880s, most silos, which were rectangular or square in shape, were inadequate and inefficient. King, a physics professor, wanted to improve upon this. He studied many different types of silos that were in use in four midwestern states. In an 1891 publication, he presented his results and plans for what became known as the King, or Wisconsin, all-wood circular silo.[1] While the design of earlier silos made them hard to pack and allowed too much spoilage, the round silos avoided these problems and offered farmers a cost savings on the construction.

King's research was not limited to silos; he also had a keen interest in barns. In January 1889, his brother, C. E. King, asked Franklin to construct a barn, including a silo, that would economically shelter eighty cows and ten horses, with feeding and cleaning alleys in front and behind. Instead of constructing a more traditional rectangular barn, Franklin decided on a 90-foot-diameter round barn with his all-wood circular silo positioned in the center. When completed, C. E. King's barn was the first of a generation of true-circular silo barns, characterized by balloon-frame construction,[2] horizontal wood siding, and a conical roof that required support posts arranged in a circular pattern around the central silo. Most of these barns had a ramp leading to the second floor. Some, however, were built as bank barns—that is, a barn built on the side, or bank, of a hill. Such a barn gave the farmer easy access to the second floor.

So successful was this plan that King promoted it in numerous agricultural publications between 1890 and 1900, including all six editions of

↖ Emery McNamee's business envelope featured a round barn he built in Regina, Saskatchewan, Canada. ENVELOPE: 1911 (Courtesy Helen [Adams] Barney, granddaughter of Emery McNamee)

↖ Emery McNamee (1858–1959) poses at the left in a picture postcard with two young men believed to be his sons, Frank and Ralph. Emery and his father, Isaac, are responsible for constructing many buildings in Henry, Rush, and Wayne counties and are credited with building the first true-circular barns in Indiana. Emery also built one of the last in 1927. POSTCARD: CA. 1911 (Courtesy Helen [Adams] Barney, granddaughter of Emery McNamee)

↖ The John Whisler barn near Warrington was one of the first true-circular barns built in Indiana and the second built by the McNamees. After it survived a 1902 tornado, it gained the reputation of being "cyclone-proof," which brought the builders instant fame. DRAWING: DATE UNKNOWN, C. A. HARTMAN (Courtesy John H. Whisler, son of original owner)

his own popular textbook on agriculture.[3] These promotions evidently reached Indiana. Two isolated examples following King's design—the Robert F. Thompson barn in Parke County and the Henry Kemp barn in Madison County—were constructed in the state before 1900.[4] But the idea did not make a real impact until several Indiana builders adopted and circulated the design. Starting in 1900 and continuing over a period of several years, these entrepreneurs would improve upon King's plan, perfect the self-supporting roof, and develop the design ultimately marketed as the Ideal Circular Barn. During this initial period, many round barns would be constructed east of Indianapolis in Delaware, Hancock, Henry, Madison, Marion, Rush, and Wayne counties. Later these men would expand their services by initiating and promoting the construction of many round barns across the Midwest and Canada. Within this seven-county area, it was the construction of two round barns thirty miles east of Indianapolis that started the enthusiasm.

William Hill was a Quaker, an experimenter, and "a man strong and serene, purposeful and able to compel."[5] In 1900, he hired local contractor Isaac McNamee of Knightstown, Indiana, and Isaac's son, Emery, of Dublin, Indiana, to construct a true-circular silo barn[6] on his farm near Carthage in northwestern Rush County. As a professor of agriculture at the University of Chicago, Hill was undoubtedly familiar with the round barns designed by Franklin King. At the time, the true-circular barn was a novel idea; no one in this region had ever constructed one. Indeed, the use of the circular silo—and even of silage—by Indiana farmers for feeding purposes was still in its infancy. Few farmers had yet constructed a silo, let alone constructed one inside a barn. Hill's was the first silo to be built in the Carthage area.[7]

No one knows why Hill picked the McNamees to build this unusual structure. In fact, very little is known about the actual construction of the Hill barn because the barn has been gone for many years, and few remember that it ever existed. But by the turn of the century, Isaac and Emery McNamee were established contractors in the area, so they were probably a logical choice to take on such an endeavor.

Isaac, born in 1832 in Akron, Ohio, was orphaned at age eight while his family was heading west via wagon train. He was taken in by John Holland, a Quaker and carpenter who resided in

◄ Benton Steele (1867–1946), the Father of Indiana's Round Barns, overcame the limitations of a third-grade education to become a skilled carpenter, draftsman, and architect. His enthusiastic promotions and regular advertisements in an Indianapolis agricultural newspaper, *The Indiana Farmer,* from 1902 to 1909 helped Indiana's round barns reach a pinnacle in construction starts in 1910. Photo: 1911, FROM FAMILY PHOTOGRAPHS COLLECTED BY LINDA J. HARSIN, GRANDDAUGHTER OF BENTON STEELE (Courtesy State Historical Society of Iowa, Historic Preservation Bureau)

⋀ Steele may have first tried his hand at carpentry in 1879, during the construction of his great-aunt's house, shown here. Perhaps this experience planted the seeds of the circular form that would later blossom in his career. Photo: 1987

Dudley Township in Henry County near New Castle. Through Holland, Isaac, and later his son Emery, learned the carpentry business and became known throughout the region.[8]

Being chosen to construct Hill's barn had an immediate impact on the McNamees. Inspired by the possibilities of the round barn, they realized that this was an opportunity to make their mark in

the world and quickly sought out other farmers willing to try this new type of barn. Soon after the Hill barn was built, they convinced John Whisler, a farmer living north of Warrington in northeastern Hancock County, to build one. Construction of the Whisler barn was important because it introduced the McNamees to another local carpenter and self-taught architect, Benton Steele. Soon the McNamees and Steele formed a loose partnership, and Steele proved to be just the man the McNamees needed to promote the round-barn concept.

Benton Steele was born in 1867 near the towns of Warrington and Willow Springs in Hancock County, about thirty miles east of Indianapolis. When he turned fourteen, his family moved to Halstead, Kansas, but he stayed behind to work for A. B. Thomas, an affluent businessman who owned the general store and managed Willow Springs's post office. Working as a huckster for Thomas, Steele probably sold general merchandise and passed mail. Sometime around 1890 he started working with wood and probably worked as a carpenter's apprentice for a local contractor. Here he learned the carpentry trade, but more importantly, he acquired a flair for drawing and became accomplished at drafting precise blueprints and plans. His expertise is clearly evident in the many beautiful, detailed drawings of round barns and other farm structures he would later present in various agricultural newspapers.[9] His experience as a draftsman and salesman made Steele the ideal man to promote the "ideal" barn.

Steele's strong interest in the circular form can probably be attributed to the octagonal house that his great-aunt, Jane Ross Reeves, had constructed near his Willow Springs home when Steele was thirteen years old. In all probability, Steele later worked for Brewster and Traher, the builders of his aunt's house. Reeves might have built her house under the influence of Orson Squire Fowler's promotion of octagonal structures in the 1850s (see pp. 6–7). Like Fowler, Steele came to advocate circular forms not only for practical but also for aesthetic or philosophical reasons. As Steele wrote in a note found at the time of his death, "The circular form of building is and always has been and always will be, the ultimate in architectural form as well as the strongest shapes ever conceived by man. The Creator made and fashioned every known or tangible thing after the circular form and to travel and function in circular or elliptical orbits . . . by reason of circular motion and because of the circular shape of all terrestrial and existing things."[10] Fowler, too, believed the circle to be the perfect design in nature, even capable of influencing one's state of mind.

The popularity of round barns also reached the circles of politics and business in the state's capital. In 1901, Indianapolis was the hub of activity for the state's livestock trade. Here farmers, bankers, politicians, and businessmen congregated from all over the state to conduct the flourishing day-to-day agricultural business. Many were wealthy, well educated, open-minded, and progressive. As they witnessed the tremendous economic expansion taking place in the Midwest, they were eager to listen to new ideas, especially to those that would save them money and increase their stature in the livestock trade and dairy business.

In early 1901, Benton Steele and Samuel "Frank" Detraz, a woodworker from Pendleton, Indiana, entered these Indianapolis business circles with a novel idea. They presented plans for a round barn that they claimed would be cheaper to build and save labor because of the conveniences the circular design offered. The plan was so unusual that it caught the eye of two prominent business-

men: Freemont Goodwine, a state senator from Warren County, the president of Williamsport State Bank, and a breeder of fine cattle; and Wymond J. Beckett, an Indianapolis lawyer, farmer, and eventual state senator.[11]

Goodwine was so impressed with the plan that he had Detraz, Steele, and probably Isaac and Emery McNamee construct an 80-foot-diameter barn with a 24-foot-diameter central silo on his farm near Williamsport.[12] Beckett, equally impressed, had the group construct a 100-foot-diameter barn on his farm near Aurora, Indiana, in Dearborn County. Beckett's enthusiasm is clearly evident in a 1902 letter to Detraz and Steele:

> My barn is now completed and I am more than pleased with it. It is the largest and finest barn in the state. There have been thousands of people to see it and all pronounce it the most convenient barn they ever saw. I have a 16-foot windmill on the roof to pump water and grind food. The circular barn is a great improvement over the rectangular plan. To give best results I think

Building Plans Should be made by Architects of long experience in a special line. Ours is PLANNING and DESIGNING "THE IDEAL CIRCULAR BARN." A barn without a fault, cheap to construct, handsome in appearance, and proof against storms. We design large buildings for any purpose requiring self supporting roof and large unobstructed floor space. Give us your ideas and we will do the rest; correspondence solicited. Best of reference and numerous testimonials. DETRAZ & STEEL, Architects, Johnson Block, Pendleton, Indiana.

➤ Two of several Detraz-Steele advertisements promoting their designs. ADVERTISEMENTS: "BUILDING PLANS," *INDIANA FARMER*, MAR. 21, 1903; AND "BARN PLANS," *FARMER'S GUIDE*, APR. 18, 1903

Barn Plans. We make a specialty of planning and designing "Circular Barns" to meet the requirements of farmers, dairymen, ranchmen and breeders. The circular formation together with our special style of construction offers the final solution to barn building—there remains no feature unprovided for. Send us your ideas and let us prepare you a sketch to prove our assertions. We also furnish working drawings for the "The Peer Silo" and the "Perfection Dehorning Stall" on short notice. Write for full particulars to **DETRAZ & STEELE, Architects, Pendleton, Ind.**

◄ Samuel Francis "Frank" Detraz (1866–1911) may have been responsible for the woodwork and many of the fancy entrances seen on the true-circular barns built in partnership with Steele from 1901 to 1904. Detraz grew up in Vevay, located in extreme southeastern Indiana, in a family of skilled carpenters. His brothers Clarence and Eugene specialized in building self-supporting spiral staircases, some of which still exist in southern Indiana homes. PHOTO: CA. 1895, J. E. WALTON (Courtesy Mildred E. Detraz, daughter-in-law of Frank Detraz)

➤ In 1902, Benton Steele was quoted in an article for Chicago's weekly agricultural journal that highlighted the Fremont Goodwine round barn in Warren County. Designed and built circa 1901, it is the first known round barn showing a double-pitched gambrel roof instead of a conical roof. This important improvement gave the farmer a tremendous increase in storage capacity in the loft. ELEVATION: FROM "A CIRCULAR BARN WITH SILO," *BREEDER'S GAZETTE*, JULY 2, 1902

CIRCULAR BARN WITH SILO

➤ A photograph of Fremont Goodwine's barn does not exist because the barn has been down for many years; however, many Indiana barns resemble it. Shown here is the Cirus Stafford barn built in 1908 in Delaware County. PHOTO: 1985

the circular barn should be built two story with a basement like mine. The roof of my barn is a perfect cone and a beauty. I can certainly recommend you and your barn very cheerfully. I think there is no plan of barn to compare with it.[13]

News of the daring new circular concept spread rapidly as word-of-mouth advertising brought many inquiries from local farmers. By the end of 1901, Steele, Detraz, and the McNamees had their hands full with the construction of the Goodwine barn in Warren County and the Beckett barn in Dearborn County.

Their expanding business allowed them to hire skilled carpenters to help with orders. One was Horace Duncan, a young carpenter from Knightstown, Indiana, who became a close associate of Isaac McNamee and would later have a major influence—both positive and negative—on the construction of round barns in the Midwest. While Duncan was growing up, he undoubtedly knew Isaac and Emery McNamee, who were also from the Knightstown area. He may have worked as their apprentice during the construction of William Hill's round barn in 1900. Duncan's first known exposure to the circular

barn occurred in 1901 when the McNamees and Steele were constructing barns in the Pendleton area. Duncan was a quick learner, and by 1902 at age twenty-five, he was responsible and skilled enough to supervise the construction of the F. W. Boettcher round barn near Artis, South Dakota.[14]

By 1902, orders from Madison County farmers were so strong that Steele moved from Warrington to Pendleton to set up headquarters with Detraz, which allowed him to be closer to Indianapolis business circles while providing good access to local farmers who wanted to build round barns. Emery McNamee set up residence in

Duncan's Type of Barn

Is the only Round Barn that is constructed entirely upon scientific principles.

Plans are strictly cash in advance. Price of plans will be returned where I personally execute the work of building barn.

Some unscrupulous, would-be architects, in order to obtain a few dollars for worthless plans, gotten up with no knowledge of circular construction, thus causing many disappointments and much extra and unexpected expense during construction, are endeavoring to make prospective builders believe that my barn is not patented. They willingly make any misleading statement. They have nothing to lose, not even a reputation.

If you are interested, or have any doubt in regard to patent, send 10 cents to Omeara & Brock, Patent Attorneys, Washington, D. C., and ask for copy of Letters Patent No. 804427, which you will promptly receive. I will promptly prosecute each and every infringer.

Pencil sketches of interior arrangement sent for approval before mak[...]

Always give an idea of the size of barn you contemplate building, an[...] ber and kinds of stock to be kept in same.

We furnish the farm right free with each set of plans. Farm rights, [...]

The following table represents the price of plans and specifications [...] all materials used in the construction of the Duncan patent barn for the [...] below:

Diameter in Feet	Square Feet of Floor Space	Price	Diameter in Feet	Square Feet of Floor Space	Price	Diameter in Feet
40	1257	$10 00	55	2376	$19 00	70
41	1320	10 55	56	2463	19 70	71
42	1385	11 10	57	2552	20 40	72
43	1452	11 60	58	2642	21 15	73
44	1520	12 16	59	2734	21 85	74
45	1590	12 70	60	2827	22 60	75
46	1663	13 30	61	2922	23 20	76
47	1746	13 90	62	3019	24 15	77
48	1809	14 45	63	3117	24 95	78
49	1886	15 10	64	3217	25 75	79
50	1963	15 70	65	3318	26 55	80
51	2043	16 35	66	3421	27 35	From 80 t
52	2124	17 00	67	3526	28 20	From 101 t
53	2205	17 65	68	3632	29 05	
54	2290	18 30	69	3739	29 90	

Ideal Circular Barn, Owned by Frank L. Middleton, McCordsville, Ind.

IDEAL CIRCULAR BARN

Benton Steele, Architect,

PENDLETON, IND.

⚑ One of Benton Steele's promotions was his pamphlet, the *Ideal Circular Barn*. Statements by Steele and testimonials and letters from prominent farmers promoting the design were featured inside the publication and the cover featured a photo of Indiana's largest round barn, the Littleton barn in Hancock County. PAMPHLET: FROM BENTON STEELE, *IDEAL CIRCULAR BARN* (PENDLETON, IND.: PRIVATELY PRINTED, CA. 1905) (Courtesy Mary Hacker, granddaughter of Elizabeth Kitchen)

⚑ Horace Duncan's letterhead featured the F. W. Boettcher barn, which was designed by Benton Steele. Boettcher, like many other early round-barn owners, was a wealthy farmer. LETTERHEAD: 1911 (Courtesy Everett Gruber, grandson of Jasper Hufty)

⚑ Horace Duncan (1877–1928) was known as the "The Round Barn Man" from Knightstown, Indiana. Although responsible for the construction of numerous circular barns in Indiana and other states, his eventual patent infringement claims may have contributed to the decline of these barns. PHOTO: 1910, PHOTOGRAPHER UNKNOWN (Courtesy Mrs. Clifford Shively, daughter of Horace Duncan)

Anderson, located a few miles away from Pendleton. This was the first of many temporary residences where Emery and his crew would move from one town to the next, building round barns. Such roving crews were not uncommon during these times. Finally, Isaac McNamee, then seventy years old, stayed close to Knightstown and handled business matters.[15]

By mid-1902 these men had constructed at least five round barns in the Pendleton, Knightstown, and Warrington areas and three more elsewhere. Local interest continued to expand rapidly, and business was good. However, the real push to make the circular barn popular came from several unrelated events that launched the new barn design into Midwest agricultural headlines and initiated the era of the circular barn in Indiana. The first and most significant event was Benton Steele's promotion of the circular concept in top midwestern agricultural newspapers. Other important factors were the tremendous storm that hit the Pendleton-Warrington area in June 1902, the construction of the Frank Littleton barn in Hancock County in 1903, and the introduction of the round barn to professors associated with the University of Illinois Agricultural Experiment Station.

Detraz and Steele, having convinced many of Indiana's most prominent farmers and politicians of the virtues of the circular form, seized the opportunity and initiated an aggressive regional promotion of their Ideal Circular Barn. In March of 1902, Steele published the first of many round-barn plans in the Indianapolis-based *Indiana Farmer*. Four months later, he published plans for his circular silo barn in the Chicago-based *Breeder's Gazette*. In that article, Steele described the design and construction of the Freemont Goodwine barn in Warren County:

> The barn is especially adapted to be used in connection with the silo on account of the shape and manner in which it is constructed. It will not require an extended explanation to convince the practical stockman of the many advantages contained in this plan, as the available floor space can be arranged to suit almost any conditions or requirements that individuals in different localities may require. The capacity of the barn is sufficient to afford feeding room, grain, silage, and roughage for 180 to 200 head of cattle, being designed for a farm of 300 to 500 acres. Owing to the matter of feeding it can be built more economically than any other style of barn with which I am familiar.[16]

These beautiful new designs caught the eye of many, and the response from midwestern farmers was immediate. As a result of these promotions, Steele, Detraz, Duncan, and the McNamees filled orders for round barns all over Indiana and as far west as South Dakota and Iowa.[17] But while Steele's promotions generated tremendous enthusiasm, the round barn also had its detractors. For instance, Steele's first promotion in the *Breeder's Gazette* also met with criticism. The *Gazette* was one of the leading agricultural newspapers of the day and its editors, particularly Joseph Wing, were considered top authorities in agriculture.

Response from *Gazette* editors summarized the positive as well as the negative aspects of the circular barn. They favored the large silo and said that there "was no question as to the strength and economy of the round barn."[18] However, *Gazette* editors brought up several design flaws that required further attention: insufficient lighting and ventilation; insufficient detail on how cattle were to be stalled; use of an outdated gutter system; lack of full information on filling the hay mow and silo; and inadequate feeding troughs and auxiliaries for the cattle.

The impact of these comments on Steele was significant. This was the first time anyone had openly criticized the round-barn concept. Instead of taking the criticism personally, Steele welcomed these comments because he was hoping the editorial response would steer him in the right direction. Steele's intention was to perfect the circular barn, which would be his claim to fame and eventually earn him the title of "Father of Indiana's Round Barns."

Fueled with these new ideas, Steele and his partner, Frank Detraz, worked on a new plan. Six months later in the February 14, 1903, issue of the *Indiana Farmer*, they presented plans for the "Ideal Circular Barn." All criticisms and suggestions outlined by the *Gazette* editors were addressed. Steele and Detraz's enthusiasm is clearly evident:

> We wish to call your attention again to the "Circular Barn" as perfected by us. . . . While the history of circular barn construction is of very recent date, we offer the complete solution of the entire problem. We have successfully met and overcome every objectional feature that has been advanced against the circular barn. . . . The most prominent features of the circular barn are as follows:
> **1.** A greater capacity, with the same amount of material used, than any other form of construction.

➤ In 1907, Benton Steele built an 80-foot-diameter round barn for George Charles in Orange County. This rare photo indicates Steele (back row, far right) hired fifteen carpenters and two helpers to construct the barn. The barn was probably constructed in less than a month. Once one of the most picturesque barns in the state, it was razed in 1974. PHOTO: 1907, PHOTOGRAPHER UNKNOWN (Courtesy Shirley Koch and Coralie Tighe, granddaughters of Benton Steele)

➤ Steele hired eleven carpenters in 1907 to help build Bruce R. Huston's 56-foot-diameter barn in Switzerland County, just across the Ohio River from Warsaw, Ky. The barn is still in excellent shape. PHOTO: 1907, PHOTOGRAPHER UNKNOWN (Courtesy Shirley Koch and Coralie Tighe, granddaughters of Benton Steele)

Emery McNamee and his crew spent much of the time on the road traveling from city to city and farm to farm, building barns along the way. During one excursion in 1913, McNamee and his crew left Indiana to build round barns near Regina in Saskatchewan, Canada. This rare picture postcard shows McNamee (third from left) posing with his traveling crew. Horace Duncan may be the man in the backseat of the car. After his stay in Canada, McNamee settled in Roundup, Montana, where he continued to build round barns. POSTCARD: 1911 (Courtesy Helen [Adams] Barney, granddaughter of Emery McNamee)

2. A vast, unobstructed mow space, there being no timbers whatever of any kind to form an obstruction, the roof being entirely self-supporting.

3. The capacity of the barn can be decreased or diminished to any required size without affecting the form of construction in the least.

4. The simplicity and ease with which hay can be stored away. By using the "Ferris" self-returning hay carrier, which operates on a circular track, the barn can be filled entirely full with great ease. . . .

5. The ease by which the plan and general arrangement can be adjusted to suit the requirements of any department of stock husbandry.

6. Great strength of roof and side walls, insuring against the dangers of heavy winds and tornadoes.

7. Graceful outline in symmetry of proportion.

8. Every principle of construction is based on science, and combines simplicity, cheapness and strength.

9. No roof to sag or settle out of shape and become unsightly.

10. No sides or ends to bulge out. Just as well talk about bulging the sides of a well-hooped barrel, for the barn is built all the way through this principle.

11. Is equally well adapted to all kinds of roofing materials, whether wood, slate or metal.[19]

Reader response was immediate, and orders for round barns increased substantially, as indicated in the 1903 letter from J. B. Conner, president of the *Indiana Farmer*, to Steele and Detraz:

Gentlemen, We have your letter requesting 25 copies of *The Farmer* of this week containing cuts of your article on [the] circular barn. We will send them to you tomorrow and will of course make no charge for them, because we are exceedingly glad to have your plans to make cuts from as there is a great deal of inquiry about barns, and moreover we believe that you have the ideal barn, both in economy and almost every other feature of construction. Hoping that you will find great success in your work, we are. Very respectfully yours.[20]

In the midst of Steele's promotional efforts, Mother Nature took a turn at promoting the round barns herself. On June 24, 1902, a terrible storm passed through an area east of Indianapolis. Hancock and Madison counties were hardest hit, with the towns of Warrington and Pendleton devastated by tornadoes. Many barns, houses, and other structures were destroyed. However, the John Whisler round barn "alone stood serene, not a shingle or board being so much as ripped from its place."[21]

Though unfortunate for many, this storm came at an opportune time for the round-barn builders because the survival of the Whisler barn brought them instant fame. Realizing that all farmers feared losing their barns to these terrible storms, Steele, Detraz, the McNamees, and Duncan capitalized on this anxiety by claiming, "Cyclones have no disastrous effect on cylindrical barns." Soon the circular barn became known as "cyclone proof," and its impact was tremendous as farmers from all over the Midwest began inquiring about this new design. In early 1903 a happy Emery McNamee claimed that "scores of the cyclone barns will be built this year."[22] This was somewhat of an exaggeration, but by the end of 1904, the group had built at least sixteen circular barns.

As more and more prominent farmers became interested in the innovative barns, a friendly keep-up-with-the-Jones rivalry began. By far, the most noteworthy rivalry was between Wymond Beckett, an attorney who had Steele build a 100-foot diameter round barn for him in 1901 on his Dearborn County farm, and his friend, Frank L. Littleton, an influential Indianapolis attorney and state representative. Littleton had a farm near McCordsville, east of Indianapolis, and in a competitive spirit, he decided not to be outdone by his friend. Soon Littleton contacted Steele and had him design a larger barn, a 102-foot-diameter monster with a 16-foot windmill in the center, so he could boast the largest round barn in the state.[23]

While the rivalry was an interesting aspect of Littleton's barn, its construction was more important for another reason: it brought together six individuals—Frank Littleton, Isaac and Emery McNamee, Benton Steele, Horace Duncan, and Frank Detraz—to build the largest round barn in the state and add important improvements to the construction of the self-supporting roof.[24] Littleton, with his legal expertise, would prove to be especially crucial to this association.

Littleton, a graduate from DePauw University with degrees in philosophy, law, and the arts, was associated with the law office of Byron K. Elliott in Indianapolis between 1896 and 1905. As a Republican, Littleton was elected to the 1896 Indiana General Assembly and became Speaker of the House of Representatives, a position he held until 1899.[25] Viewing the round barn as a novel idea and an opportunity to expand his stature in the community, Littleton teamed up

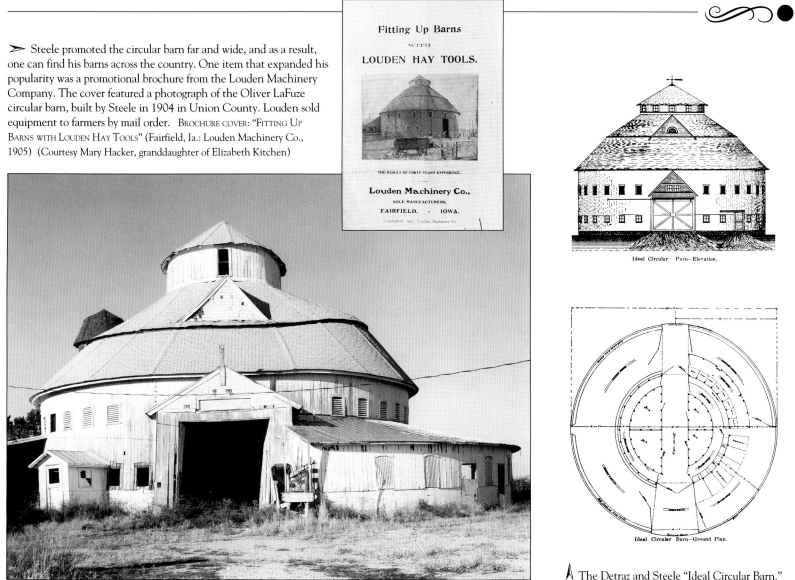

Steele promoted the circular barn far and wide, and as a result, one can find his barns across the country. One item that expanded his popularity was a promotional brochure from the Louden Machinery Company. The cover featured a photograph of the Oliver LaFuze circular barn, built by Steele in 1904 in Union County. Louden sold equipment to farmers by mail order. BROCHURE COVER: "FITTING UP BARNS WITH LOUDEN HAY TOOLS" (Fairfield, Ia.: Louden Machinery Co., 1905) (Courtesy Mary Hacker, granddaughter of Elizabeth Kitchen)

Fitting Up Barns
WITH
LOUDEN HAY TOOLS.

THE RESULT OF FORTY YEARS EXPERIENCE.

Louden Machinery Co.,
SOLE MANUFACTURERS.
FAIRFIELD, - IOWA.

Copyrighted, 1905, Louden Machinery Co.

Ideal Circular Barn—Elevation.

Ideal Circular Barn—Ground Plan.

Ʌ Steele and Detraz responded to criticism of their round-barn design by introducing the "Ideal Circular Barn." Later that year, Steele, Detraz, Duncan, and the McNamees built a barn that closely resembled the improved design for Dr. Horace Jones of Summitville in northern Madison County. PHOTO: 1987

Ʌ The Detraz and Steele "Ideal Circular Barn." ELEVATION AND FLOOR PLAN: FROM DETRAZ AND STEELE, "THE CIRCULAR IDEAL BARN" [*sic*], INDIANA FARMER, FEB. 14, 1903

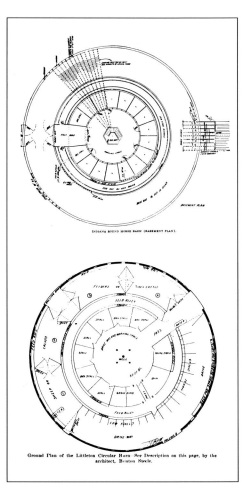

≺ Wymond J. Beckett's 100-foot-diameter true-circular barn (top left) was the largest in the state until Frank Littleton built a 102-foot version on his farm in Hancock County. Today, these round barns are still the largest in the state. PHOTO, BECKETT BARN: 1988 PHOTO, LITTLETON BARN: 1978, GEORGE GOULD

➤ The floor plans of Beckett's (top right) and Littleton's round barns were designed by Steele. Both plans feature water wells in the center and central ventilation shafts. Littleton's barn, built two years after the Beckett barn, is more complex in design, suggesting an evolution of the round-barn concept. FLOOR PLAN, BECKETT BARN: FROM BENTON STEELE, "A CIRCULAR BARN," INDIANA FARMER, JAN. 9, 1904 FLOOR PLAN, LITTLETON BARN: BENTON STEELE, "AN INDIANA ROUND HORSE BARN," IN FARM BUILDINGS (CHICAGO: BREEDER'S GAZETTE, 1913)

with Isaac McNamee and Duncan. Using his political power and legal training, he helped prepare and apply for the patent "Self-supporting Conical Roof" in November 1904.[26] The trio's efforts were rewarded in late 1905 when the patent was approved.

The patent was worded in a way that appeared to give McNamee and Duncan the almost exclusive right to build a round barn. The patent detailed the construction of several important aspects of the barn, namely the foundation, the walls, and more importantly, the construction of the self-supporting roof. Holding the patent gave the inventors some validity to claims that the idea was a sound and good investment. As a result, the patent helped convince some skeptical farmers to build a round barn instead of a rectangular one.

For unknown reasons, Steele, the architect of the Littleton barn, and his partner, Detraz, were left out of the patent, an omission which led to the eventual dissolution of the Steele-Detraz partnership. There is no mention of Detraz after 1903 in agricultural journals, newspapers, or legal documents; he probably dropped out of the round-barn construction business altogether. Steele, however, continued his relationship with Isaac McNamee. Steele was eventually a victim of Duncan's ambition, but, for the time being, he kept up with his barn-building activities, advertising in the *Indiana Farmer* and continuing to be a major influence in round-barn construction. Orders were still increasing rapidly, and business flourished.

Despite the tireless efforts of Indiana's round-barn builders, many still viewed the design as an experiment or an architectural oddity that only wealthy farmers could afford. In particular, the early promotional efforts by Steele and the other builders suffered from the lack of authoritative support from agricultural universities. In an attempt to change this, Steele and Detraz probably contacted Purdue and Indiana universities some time in 1902, but the builders' ideas did not find any interest. Undeterred, the two men sought out other authoritative sources. In 1903, their search ended when Professor C. B. Dorsey of the

≺ Frank L. Littleton (1868–1935). After his barn was completed in 1903, Littleton helped Isaac McNamee and Horace Duncan patent the roof design. His involvement with the co-inventors was apparently superficial once the patent was approved. As a partner, he probably collected royalties from farmers for the right to build a round barn. PHOTO: FROM THE AMERICAN BIOGRAPHICAL SOCIETY, *INDIANAPOLIS MEN OF AFFAIRS*, (INDIANAPOLIS, IND.: PAUL DONALD BROWN, 1923)

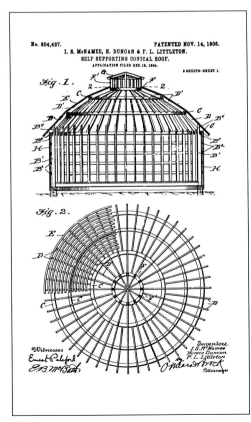

≺ The 1905 patent "Self-supporting Conical Roof" by inventors Isaac McNamee, Horace Duncan, and Frank Littleton was an improvement on the circular barn design, not a new invention as they led everybody to believe. This deception was used by Duncan to convince prospective buyers that he had the exclusive right to build true-circular barns. The patent discussed the walls, the pitched gambrel roof, and how they were connected to the purlin plates. Purlin plates (shown as C in figures 1 and 2) are composed of six 1 inch by 6 inch by 10 foot boards nailed together and bent into shape. Green wood or water-soaked lumber was used to ease the bending process. Depending on the size of the barn, three or four plates of different diameters were hoisted into place and used as a means to permanently fasten the rafters together. The plates were instrumental in allowing the roof to support itself without the use of interior posts. ELEVATION AND BARN PLAN: FROM "SELF-SUPPORTING CONICAL ROOF," U.S. PATENT 804,427, NOV. 14, 1905

➤ These two cross sections (figures 3 and 4) show how the roof rafters (*D*) are connected to the vertical studs (*B'*) through the use of a purlin plate (*B3*). The studding beams (*B'*) have a projecting portion (*B4*) that extends above the plane of the first plate (*C*). Each stud is secured to this projection and to one of the lowermost series of rafters(*D*). BARN PLAN: FROM "SELF-SUPPORTING CONICAL ROOF," U.S. PATENT 804,427, NOV. 14, 1905

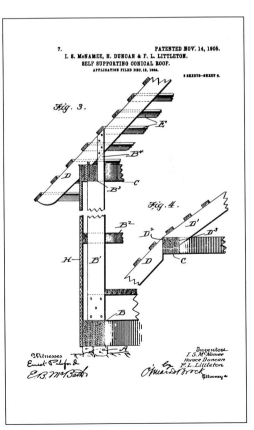

> Two of Steele's many promotions. ADVERTISE-
MENTS: "BUILDING PLANS," INDIANA FARMER, MAY 30, 1908;
AND "ROUND BARNS," INDIANA FARMER, FEB. 13, 1904

Indiana's round-barn builders gained credibility for their designs when the Agricultural Experiment Station at the University of Illinois built these three barns on campus and published *Economy of the Round Dairy Barn*.
PHOTO: FROM WILBER J. FRASER, "THE ROUND BARN," CIRCULAR 230, REVISION OF BULLETIN 143 (URBANA, ILL.: UNIVERSITY OF ILLINOIS AGRICULTURAL EXPERIMENT STATION, SEPT. 1918)

University of Illinois Agricultural Experiment Station accepted an invitation to visit the Pendleton area "to make a personal examination of the merits of the Detraz and Steele round barn." Dorsey was reportedly "highly pleased, and said that the methods of barn-building employed by [them] was a revelation to him." Later that summer, Steele and Detraz constructed a large dairy barn on Dorsey's farm in Gilberts, Illinois.[27]

Dorsey's interest in circular barns apparently caught the eye of other university professors. In 1908, the University of Illinois Dairy Department, under the direction of Wilber J. Fraser, planned the first of three barns on the campus at Champaign in east-central Illinois, using the "experience of a carpenter who makes a specialty of building round barns."[28] Two years later, the University of Illinois Agricultural Experiment Station published the widely distributed *Economy of the Round Dairy Barn*, which included detailed plans and building instructions.[29]

Through the University of Illinois, Steele and the other builders finally received the institutional support needed to push the round-barn concept to its greatest height. The publication of *Economy of the Round Dairy Barn* coincided with the peak of circular-barn construction in 1910, when at least fifteen round barns were built in Indiana. But the enthusiasm would not last. The circular-barn era, which took two decades to fully blossom, would wither away before another decade passed.

Decline of the Round Barn, 1910–18

Although *Economy of the Round Dairy Barn* represented an official endorsement of the round-barn concept, interest in round barns declined in Indiana and other Midwestern states within years of its publication. At peak construction, nineteen barns were built in 1910. Eleven were built in 1914, but by 1918, construction of these structures had virtually stopped. Even a 1918 reprint of *Economy of the Round Dairy Barn* was not able to revive interest.

Although the beginning of World War I certainly affected the decline in construction, there are other reasons why the interest in these

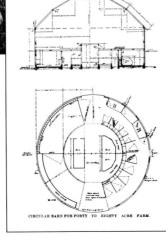

∧ Recent view of the Rankin round barn. PHOTO: 1987

CIRCULAR BARN FOR FORTY TO EIGHTY ACRE FARM.

∨ This family portrait of the Rebecca Rankin family was taken during the construction of their 50-foot-diameter circular barn in Jay County. Round barns, considered a status symbol, were often used as a backdrop for family portraits.
PHOTO: 1908 (Courtesy Tom Elliott, grandson of Rebecca Rankin)

≺ Prior to 1905, most round barns were built by wealthy farmers who could afford to take a chance on a new type of farm building; however, by 1905 there was a growing demand for medium-size barns at a reduced cost for smaller farms and, more importantly, designed for the general farmer. Benton Steele promoted the smaller, more economical barn in a December 1905 issue of the *Indiana Farmer*. Here he boasted that the plan "has been duplicated many times at a cost ranging . . . from $450 to $600." This promotion apparently convinced Elizabeth Kitchen of White County to build one, since the barn she built closely matches the one described in the article.
ELEVATION AND FLOOR PLAN: BENTON STEELE, "CIRCULAR BARN FOR FORTY TO EIGHTY ACRE FARM," *INDIANA FARMER*, DEC. 30, 1905

structures diminished. One is that agricultural expansion and farm construction throughout the entire Midwest was slowing down.[30] Most of the farms had been established, and most of the tillable land was already under cultivation. Construction in small midwestern towns had also reached its peak and was tapering off.

Moreover, the editors of the *Indiana Farmer* rarely, if ever, criticized the round barn in the early years of its construction. Consequently, farmers who built their barns before 1910 may not have been aware of some of the barn's disadvantages. After 1909, when the *Farmer's Guide* took over the lead from the *Indiana Farmer* in promoting the barns, the editors often discussed the pros and cons of the design, leaving the farmer to decide whether or not to build one. In general, the best arguments for the round barn were that less material was used to enclose the same amount of

interior space and that the round barn was thought to be stronger and more convenient. However, many farmers believed the disadvantages outweighed the advantages. They thought the circular silo barn was inconvenient to fill and that there was wasted space, especially if the interior arrangements were in rectangular form. Other problems often cited were that it was difficult to secure proper ventilation and that the center of the barn was often poorly lit, which was objectionable in a dairy barn. Finally, many farmers met considerable difficulty in securing a carpenter experienced in round-barn construction.[31]

Given these disadvantages alone, it is no wonder the round barn remained an architectural oddity and declined in popularity. But the same men who initiated the circular-barn boom in Indiana were at least partly to blame for the somewhat abrupt end to this type of construction.

Success for the individual builders was based on a team working together; when self-interest and rivalry among the builders developed, their energies were dissipated and promotion of the barn itself was forgotten. By 1911, all of the original builders had left Indiana or had passed away.

The event that saw all the prominent builders—the McNamees, Benton Steele, Horace Duncan, and Frank Detraz—working together on

Λ One of a few known promotions by Duncan.
ADVERTISEMENT: *FARMER'S GUIDE*, MAR. 30, 1907

➤ Duncan's business envelope featured a photograph of the magnificent barn he built for J. H. Manchester of Dublin, Ohio. The statement "Beware of unscrupulous architects" was probably directed toward Benton Steele, indicating the turmoil between the two carpenters. The irony is that Duncan was probably the unscrupulous one. A 1911 letter written by Steele indicates that he was probably the architect of the barn shown in the picture. ENVELOPE: 1911 (Courtesy Mary Hacker, granddaughter of Elizabeth Kitchen)

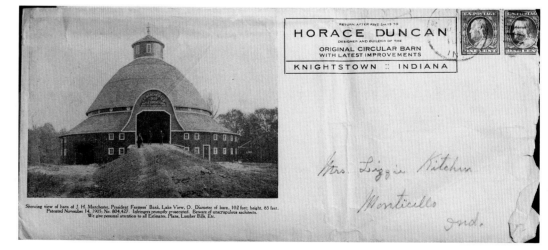

Showing view of barn of J. H. Manchester, President Farmers' Bank, Lake View, O. Diameter of barn, 102 feet; height, 85 feet. Patented November 14, 1905; No. 804,427. Infringers promptly prosecuted. Beware of unscrupulous architects. We give personal attention to all Estimates, Plans, Lumber Bills, Etc.

RETURN AFTER FIVE DAYS TO
HORACE DUNCAN
DESIGNER AND BUILDER OF THE
ORIGINAL CIRCULAR BARN
WITH LATEST IMPROVEMENTS
KNIGHTSTOWN :: INDIANA

Mrs. Lizzie Kitchen
Monticello
Ind.

their most important project was the construction of the Littleton barn in 1903. This same job sowed the seeds of discord, for Littleton helped Duncan and Isaac McNamee obtain a patent for the round barn. Duncan had, indeed, contributed several ideas to improve the self-supporting roof later patented,[32] but it is not clear why Detraz and Steele were left out of the patent or whether they were even aware that McNamee and Duncan were trying to obtain it.

Throughout the development of the round barn, Steele had been a prime mover in promotional activities. He had advertised regularly in the *Indiana Farmer*, the state's foremost agricultural newspaper. Steele left Indiana for Kansas in February 1909, just one month after the death of Isaac McNamee, although business had never been better. That Horace Duncan's activities were responsible for Steele's departure is evident.

Duncan, it is believed, wanted to be compensated for circular barns constructed by builders other than himself or one of the McNamees. Since he had patent rights, Duncan felt that all farmers and builders, including Steele, should pay a fee for the right to use his plans.[33] Steele fought this and was apparently successful as long as he maintained his working relationship with Isaac McNamee. Steele likely argued that if it were not for his promotions and advertisements, the boom in construction never would have amounted to anything. He may have also pointed out that many of the barns Duncan built were a direct result of Steele's advertisements and contacts. So from 1905 to 1909, the year of Isaac McNamee's death, Steele continued promoting and building round barns without recourse from Duncan. During this time, however, the two men argued on a regular basis, with Isaac McNamee acting as mediator.[34]

After McNamee's death, Duncan probably placed more pressure on Steele by claiming infringements to his patent and threatening legal action if he was not compensated. Without McNamee to keep the peace, Steele apparently decided to move to Kansas in order to distance him from Duncan.

The impact on the round-barn business in Indiana was immediate and tremendous. In Kansas, Steele continued to advertise in publications such as the *Kansas Farmer*, *Hoard's Dairyman*, and the *Breeder's Gazette*, but his advertisements in Indiana publications stopped abruptly. Without Steele's input, the editors of the *Indiana Farmer* quickly lost interest in round barns, and their support for the structures diminished considerably.[35] Although there were scattered promotions by other round-barn builders in the *Indiana Farmer* before and after 1909, none came close to matching the enthusiasm, persistence, quantity, and quality of

⋀ View of the J. H. Manchester barn during its construction. Photo: 1908 (Courtesy Andreas Brown Collection, Resource Collections of the Getty Center for the History of Art and the Humanities)

Steele's promotions. The result was fewer construction starts in Indiana.

After Steele's departure, Duncan stayed in Indiana. By this time, there were other round-barn builders in the state—those who learned how to build circular barns either from Steele[36] or from plans published in other agricultural publications, including *Economy of the Round Dairy Barn*. Realizing that he was losing business, Duncan compiled a list of all known round-barn owners and builders in Indiana and other states. He spent much of his time after 1909 contacting them, claiming patent infringements and demanding compensation. In Indiana, one case is documented.

In 1906, Benton Steele sold a set of circular-barn blueprints to Elizabeth Kitchen of White County. She hired James Malone, a local contractor from Buffalo, Indiana, and soon after he completed a 60-foot-diameter barn for her. Lizzie Kitchen was proud of her barn and expressed great satisfaction with it. It had "a finely cemented floor, a six barrel water tank, a driveway through the center with great sliding doors, a corn crib, two granaries, eight stalls for horses, 16 stanchions for cattle [and] convenient roomy halls for feeding stock."[37] However, Kitchen's enthusiasm was soon dampened. In 1911, she received a letter from Horace Duncan that must have come as quite a shock:

> Before placing my next list of infringers in the hands of my attorney, I give you an equal chance with others. I realize that a great many have built barns infringing on my patent with no intention of wrongdoing and for this reason I write you this letter. Had you applied to me in the start for a farm right my price would have been $25.00. If you see fit at this time to buy a right, price will be the same, otherwise I must protect my interests and will [be] proud to collect the amount allotted me by law. List will be placed in . . . [my] attorney's hands Feb. 1, 1911.[38]

Shocked, Kitchen quickly wrote and explained the situation to Benton Steele, who had settled in Halstead, Kansas. Steele responded by asking her to write Duncan and "ask him who planned the barn shown on his letterhead and who secured the job as foreman, for him on this work, and if he had the patent at this time. Thus if he bothers you any more, let me know promptly. You should, however, pay no attention to him whatever."[39] Although it is not documented, Kitchen apparently took Steele's advice and Duncan left her alone. Other barn owners may not have been so lucky though.

The effect Duncan's activities had on construction starts may never be known because the popularity of the round barn was already declining due to its inherent disadvantages (see p. 28). But it is likely that the word about Duncan spread, making farmers hesitant about considering a round barn or carpenters apprehensive about entering into the business. Those who did not want to be bothered by Duncan went around him by building barns with six, eight, ten, twelve, fourteen, or sixteen sides instead of the true-circular barn. This would explain the increase in construction of these types of barns after Duncan's 1905 patent.

Sometime in late 1911, Duncan left Indiana to pursue interests in Illinois, where *Economy of the Round Dairy Barn* had generated sales of circular barns. It is believed that he continued to construct circular barns[40] as well as to claim infringements on his patent. In 1918, when there were virtually no round barns started, Duncan returned to Indiana and continued to claim patent infringements, but his barn-building days were over.[41]

Post-1910 Construction Efforts

When Steele left Indiana in 1909, the *Farmer's Guide*, Indiana's second largest agricultural newspaper, took over round-barn promotions. Unlike the *Indiana Farmer*, which had latched on to Steele for his expertise, the *Farmer's Guide* did not rely on one major promoter or contributor. Instead, it published many designs from one-time contributors. Since the paper was a northern Indiana publication based in Huntington, this partly explains why round-barn construction starts shifted from central to northern Indiana after 1910 (see figure 3, p. 4).

Unlike the pre-1910 construction efforts by Steele, Duncan, and the McNamees, who traveled extensively across the state, the post-1910 construction period was characterized by local carpenters building circular barns in their home county or in nearby counties. This trend resulted in clusters of barns built by the same carpenter. The most notable of these builders are the Kindigs of Fulton County. If it were not for them, the round-barn construction era in Indiana would have died out much sooner than it did.

Charles Vallandingham "Lan" Kindig (1863–1940) was born in Henry Township in Fulton County, Indiana. He was raised in a family of

◅ Charles Vallandingham Kindig (front row, left) and his wife, Hattie (front row, right), pose for a portrait with their family. Their son Cleon stands between them. Other sons and daughters pictured in the back row (from left to right) are Arnie, Doris, Lavonne, Roy, Audrey, Cleve ("Pete"), and Oral ("Hap"). After Indiana's primary round-barn builders left the state between 1909 and 1913, Charles and his sons Pete, Roy, and Hap kept the circular-barn era alive in Indiana until 1923. PHOTO: CA. 1920, PHOTOGRAPHER UNKNOWN (Courtesy Eva Kindig, wife of Hap Kindig; and Pat Zehr, granddaughter of Hap Kindig)

carpenters who were responsible for the construction of many buildings in the Fulton-Miami-Kosciusko county area. Charles married young and had eight children. Three of them—Cleve "Pete" (1886–1961), Roy (1889–1968), and Oral "Hap" (1897–1975)—eventually joined their father and formed C. V. Kindig and Sons. The trio built many of the schools and churches, and hundreds of houses, barns, chicken sheds, and corn cribs in a three-county area. The Kindigs were successful; they never had to advertise because their reputation brought them plenty of business.[42]

By 1910, many Indiana farmers had heard of the Ideal Circular Barn, and, for one reason or another, the idea really caught on in the Fulton County area. Since the Kindigs were the prime contractors in the county, they were the logical choice to build the round barns. The Kindigs built

their first circular barn around 1910, coinciding with the publication of the *Economy of the Round Dairy Barn* by the University of Illinois.

The Kindigs considered the round barn to be structurally inferior to the rectangular barn, but they built round barns because of the demand for them.[43] In all, they built at least twenty-three round barns, or about 20 percent of the circular barns built in Indiana after 1910. Their handiwork comprises the largest cluster of round barns in Indiana and perhaps the United States, a fact that is celebrated by the Fulton County Round Barn Festival held every summer.

Adding to the decline of the round barn was the apparent lack of support by Purdue University, Indiana's premier agricultural school. Unlike the University of Illinois, which openly promoted round barns, Purdue had little to do with the idea.

Purdue's agricultural publications were mainly concerned with improvements in farm produce. Of the little that was written on farm structures, nothing was published concerning round barn construction.[44] However, in 1939 a Purdue publication appropriately described the fate of these barns: "Many barns had unusual features built to suit the whims of the owner. Round or hexagonal shape, excessively large cupolas, driveways . . . are just a few examples. While these peculiarities may have made the barn more satisfactory to the original owner, they sometimes made it less suited to succeeding users." Most circular barns and their rectangular cousins "lacked the adaptability to different uses without excessive expense for changing. A barn originally constructed to fill a definite need and well suited to do that need, may become unsuited to future needs through changes in

➤ The Ora Tucker barn built in 1913 in Kosciusko County was one of at least twenty-three round barns built by the Kindigs. The barn burned down in 1975.
PHOTO: CA. 1913, PHOTOGRAPHER UNKNOWN (Courtesy Winifred [Tucker] Smith, daughter of Ora Tucker)

conditions, changes in operator, or changes in type of farming. Extreme differences from the tried and accepted features often decreased the value of the barn's future use or sale."[45]

That thought generally still holds true. Many barns today—round as well as some rectangular—are obsolete. They are too small to handle today's farm equipment. Most of the remaining round barns are either abandoned or used for storage. Often owners strip the barn of its cow stanchions, manure tracks, and other items of historic value. Recently, however, there seems to be a small movement to save some of these old structures. After all, round barns are not only unusual but also aesthetically pleasing.

◄ Interior view of the John Haimbaugh barn built by the Kindigs in Fulton County. At the time of the barn's construction in 1914, the cow stanchions, poured-concrete floor, gutter system, and manure track were state-of-the-art equipment.
PHOTO: 1985

A Multitude of Designs

*T*here is truth to the old saying "No two barns are alike." Barns were built to satisfy the individual needs of the farmer, and each farmer's needs differed from those of his neighbor. Benton Steele, Horace Duncan, and others realized this when promoting their services and plans. When considering plans, the farmer was asked to describe individual needs. The architect would then take these ideas and prepare preliminary sketches outlining the barn plan. The two would confer, and eventually a final plan would be prepared. Items always taken into consideration were the size of the farm; the number of work horses, cattle, and other livestock; and the number of stanchions required for dairy purposes.

Budgeting was a major concern because many of the farmer's options involved additional costs.

◄ Indiana's round barns come in various shapes and sizes, such as the Oliver Hardy barn, built circa 1916 in Scott County. The barn was razed in 1990. PHOTO: 1987

33

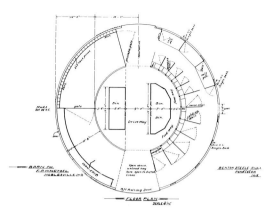

Obviously, the larger the barn, the more expensive it was. And there were other considerations. Would it be a bank barn? Would there be a silo? Would the floor consist of poured concrete or dirt? Would there be a circular hay track in the roof? Features such as the roof type, the number of windows, extra wide doors, or a large cupola for more light increased the cost. Working in this manner enabled the builders to market their ideas, especially to prominent farmers who wanted showplace farms. But the architect did not forget the small farmer. Since most farmers couldn't afford expensive barns or only required small barns, the designer had basic plans to fit the small farmer's needs, too. But even these plans differed from each other in many respects. The end result was a multitude of designs, where every barn, though quite similar in some respects, ended up a little different from the others, even if constructed from the same plan.

➤ The Floyd Whetsal barn (above) in Hamilton County and the Elizabeth Kitchen barn in White County were built from the same blueprints. The result was two barns that resembled one another but reflected individual character as well. PHOTO, WHETSAL BARN: DATE AND PHOTOGRAPHER UNKNOWN (Courtesy Nelle Hoss) PHOTO, KITCHEN BARN: 1987

Note: Keep this bill at home and copy one for saw mill men. It may save you no end of worry.

Lumber Bill For E. V. Kitchen
Monticello Ind.

Barn 60 ft in diameter 20 ft to plate.

84	Pieces	2×6″ – 20 ft. long	studds 28″ O.C.
84	″	2×5 – 16′ ″	First-breal Rafters one to each
84	″	2×5 – 14′6″ ″	2d ″
23	″	2×4 – 12′ ″	Cut into studs for ventilator
26	″	2×4 – 11′ ″	Rafters on ventilator
84	″	2×7 – 15′ ″	Outer span mow joist one at each stud
40	″	2×7 – 12′ ″	Inner ″
16	″	2×7 – 10′ ″	Joist over driveway. 2′ O.C.
14	″	2×7 – 16′ ″	braces over driveway
16	″	2×5 – 12′ ″	Sill joist & on on left side
18	″	2×8 – 14′ ″	Right ″
40	″	2×4 – 16′ ″	For general use inside.
14	″	4×4 – 12 ft	Short stall manger posts
120	″	4×4 – 11′ ″	Studs at either side of driveway
30	″	4×4 – 8′ ″	″ at front line of mangers
110	″	2×6 – 14′ ″	Cut into for crib joist & c
50	″	1×5 – 12′ ″	Jols, doors, stalls & c
4	″	1×10 – 16′6″ ″	for headers over big doors
4	″	1×10 – 14′ ″	

1000 ft. 1×2½″ for crib lath & rack strips
25 pieces 2×3 to cut into to form upright rack pieces.
1,500 ft. Board measure for stall lining mangers & c
1,050 Lineal feet 1×6 for main sill 6 members

1,440	″	″	¾×6 story plate 6 members
1,900	″	″	1×4 ″ nail ties doubled
1,000	″	″	¾×5 Inner sill joist braces
550	″	″	¾×6 Joist braces at front of mangers
960	″	″	2×6 2d purline posts 7 members
900	″	″	1½×6 Ventilator sill & last roof plate
5,200	″	″	1×1½ Roof sheathing on main roof
2,550	″	″	1×1½ ″ smaller circle
750	″	″	1×1 ″ on ventilator

Roof sheathing should be of some soft fibrous wood and balance of bill should be of any kind of native timber

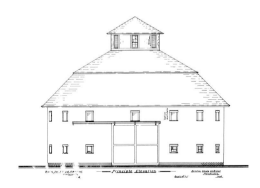

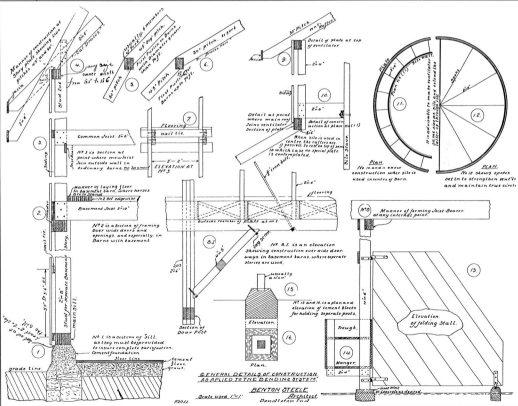

◄ The blueprints and instructions used to build the Whetsal and Kitchen barns (partially shown here) were prepared by Benton Steele and sold by mail order. All that was needed was the lumber and a competent carpenter. BUILDING PLANS: 1904 (Courtesy Mary Hacker, granddaughter of Elizabeth Kitchen)

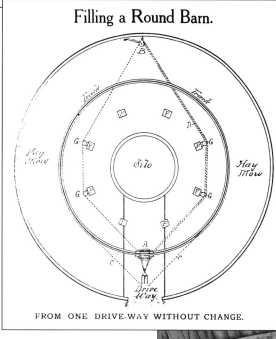

Filling a Round Barn.

FROM ONE DRIVE-WAY WITHOUT CHANGE.

➤ From 1903 to 1920, Benton Steele was associated with Louden Machinery Company of Fairfield, Iowa. The company specialized in producing labor-saving farm devices and sold them to farmers across the Midwest. One such device was the circular hay track, which was used for loading hay into the mow of a round barn. In Louden's 1905 brochure, "Fitting Up Barns with Louden Hay Tools," Steele explains how it works:

"This plan shows how a round barn can be filled from one point all the way around without change. The hay is taken up at A and the hoisting rope is run around rollers G' on the posts P, to the pulley B, and then down to the horse. The rollers G are made long enough to catch the slack of the rope, or it may be provided with guards to prevent it from getting below them. Where there are no posts the rollers are mounted in frames secured to the roof or to overhead timbers.

"When the carrier is back on the track near B, it can be drawn around on the left hand side in place of the right. This is all the change that is needed to fill both sides all around the barn. A Swivel Carrier should be used. When the track is a complete circle only one stop at A is required. It may, however, be separated at this point and run out in the driveway, as shown by the dotted lines C. In this case two stops for the carrier will be required."

HAY TRACK DIAGRAM: "FITTING UP BARNS WITH LOUDEN HAY TOOLS" (FAIRFIELD, IA.: LOUDEN MACHINERY CO., 1905) (Courtesy Mary Hacker, granddaughter of Elizabeth Kitchen)

Shown here is an example of a circular hay track inside a Marshall County barn built for George Ramsey in 1911. Note the excellent view of the circular purlin plates. PHOTO: 1986

Round barns appealed to farmers because the farmer got more for the money with a round barn than with a rectangular one. In a December 1906 issue of the *Indiana Farmer*, Steele compared the circular barn with its rectangular counterpart and discussed the potential savings. Shown is a plan for a 32x54-foot rectangular barn with a perimeter of 172 linear feet and an area of 1,728 square feet. The circular barn plan at 55 feet in diameter also has a perimeter of 172 linear feet, yet it contains an area of 2,365 square feet. This difference of 637 square feet can be doubled to an astonishing 1,274 square feet when the mow floor is added in. Hence, it was argued the round barn was the more economical of the two designs.

The circular barn plan shown here is unique. Generally, most plans are of two types: a silo barn or a barn with a central drive through it. This design is a combination of both. It has a central silo and a central drive that skirts around the silo on one side. Two Indiana barns were constructed using this plan. The barns were built around 1909 for Albert Leroy Keesling in Delaware County by Horace Duncan, and both are still standing. The one shown here was built first. Note how the left entrance has been walled up. FLOOR PLANS: FROM BENTON STEELE, "TWO BARNS COMPARED," *INDIANA FARMER*, DEC. 15, 1906 PHOTO: 1985

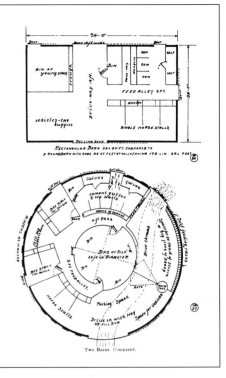

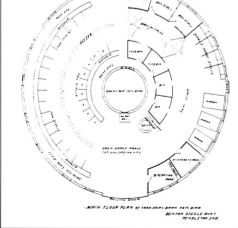

A Steele wrote in a 1905 issue of the *Indiana Farmer:* "The sketch on this page shows a circular barn 72 feet in diameter which was planned with special reference to the needs of dairy farmers, where a few head of cattle and work horses can be kept, along with feed, the wagons, the milk room, sparing room for a few nursing cows and calves, at the same time keep the dairy herd pretty well separated from the balance of the livestock, which seems to be a desired feature among most dairymen." Emery McNamee built a 76-foot-diameter barn following this design for Jim Sears of Pendleton around 1902. FLOOR PLAN: FROM BENTON STEELE, "FARM DAIRY BARN," *INDIANA FARMER,* JAN. 14, 1905 PHOTO: 1985

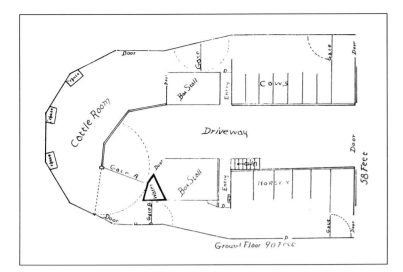

Ground Floor Plot

V Many people who travel Indiana State Road 37 south of Huntington are familiar with this landmark, but few know the history of the S. C. Snyder barn. The rectangular portion was built in 1904, and two years later it was remodeled by adding a half-circular barn on the south side. Its construction is an ideal example of a farmer's ingenuity and skill. Snyder designed the barn and completed the carpentry and cement work himself. "He had no previous apprenticeship work in either, but having the will to do a thing, the accomplishment was not difficult," according to a 1908 article in *Farmer's Guide*.

FLOOR PLAN: FROM "A REMODELED BARN," *FARMER'S GUIDE*, JULY 11, 1908   PHOTO: 1985

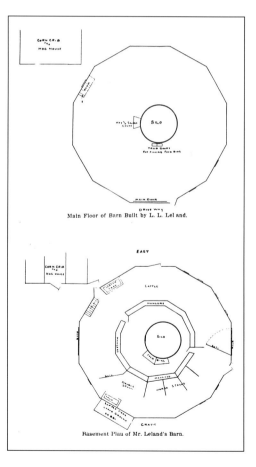

Main Floor of Barn Built by L. L. Leland.

Basement Plan of Mr. Leland's Barn.

Ⱥ During 1912 and 1913, Lawson L. Leland built three 12-sided bank barns on his family's farms in Marshall County. In the May 30, 1914, issue of the *Farmer's Guide*, Leland described and presented plans for the first of the three: "This barn can be built cheaper than a square or rectangular barn of the same size as it takes less than two-thirds as much frame, less foundation wall, siding, paint and roofing." Shown is Leland's first twelve-sided barn as it appeared in 1914 and in 1987. FLOOR PLANS AND PHOTO, TOP RIGHT: FROM "A TWELVE SIDED BARN," *FARMER'S GUIDE*, MAY 30, 1914 PHOTO, TOP LEFT: 1987

Located in Lake County in northwestern Indiana, Edward and Julias Echterling's twin circular barns and circular house are one of the most unusual landmarks in the state. Built by Horace Duncan in 1909 and 1910, one was a horse barn and the other was a dairy barn. The house was built shortly after the two barns. FLOOR PLANS: FROM EDWARD ECHTERLING, "PRACTICAL ROUND BARNS," *FARMER'S GUIDE*, MAY 18, 1912   PHOTO: 1988

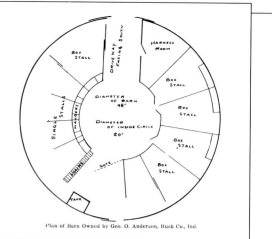

Plan of Barn Owned by Geo. O. Anderson, Rush Co., Ind.

◄ In 1906 George Anderson hired Horace Duncan to build a 48-foot-diameter round barn on his farm in Rush County. Later, in a 1911 *Farmer's Guide* article, Anderson presented a plan and description for the barn. He wrote, "The loft of this barn contains three bins for oats, bran and shipstuff. Chutes come down from bins near the water tank and the box stalls. Hay and corn are fed from the loft. The estimated capacity of the mow is seventy-five tons of hay. The hay is taken up from the outside at the four-foot door and runs up to the highest point in the barn. No need for a man in the mow. The fork after it is started back runs almost by it-self." FLOOR PLAN: FROM "PRACTICAL BARN PLANS," *FARMER'S GUIDE*, APR. 8, 1911 PHOTO: 1985

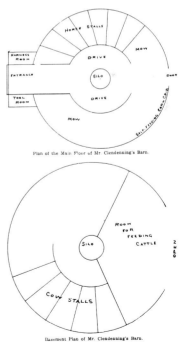

Plan of the Main Floor of Mr. Clendenning's Barn.

Basement Plan of Mr. Clendenning's Barn.

Λ J. Seymour Clendenning's bank barn in Clinton County was touted as one of the largest in Indiana when it was built in 1912. At 66 feet in diameter, it is not the widest, but its 70-foot height certainly makes it one of the tallest. Its unusual domed roof and attractive entrance make the Clendenning barn one of the most beautiful in Indiana.   FLOOR PLANS: FROM "A BIG ROUND BARN," *FARMER'S GUIDE*, SEPT. 6, 1913
PHOTO: 1987

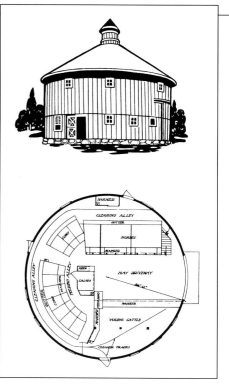

◁ In a February 1912 issue of the *Farmer's Guide*, F. L. Marsh, an authority on farm buildings, presented an elevation and plan of a 48-foot-diameter barn. When responding to a question about why the circular barn was the best and cheapest, Marsh answered: "You know the old rule that a circle will enclose more space with a given length of line than any other figure. It is therefore plain that you get the most for your money and it is the actual fact that the final cost of a round barn is less than that of a rectangular barn with the same floor and storage space."

In Indiana, the only barn resembling Marsh's design is the George Price barn in Rush County. Built in 1911 by Frank Russ Tweedy of Carthage, Indiana, the barn still stands today in an attractive farm setting.   ELEVATION AND FLOOR PLAN: FROM "MONEY SAVING ROUND BARN," *FARMER'S GUIDE*, FEB. 10, 1912 PHOTO: 1985

▼ Chicago Wrecking House's barn design no. 206 closely resembles the Maria and Franklin Wiltrout fourteen-sided barn built in DeKalb County in 1910. This design was advertised in various agricultural newspapers from 1910 to 1913. Chicago Wrecking House began business after the Chicago Fire of 1871, when there was a need to demolish burned houses. Later the company expanded and sold prefabricated houses and barns.   PHOTO: 1985

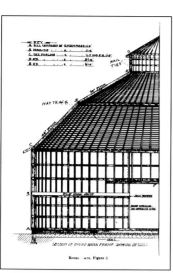

The Loni Dyson barn in Wells County follows a design that Benton Steele submitted in a September 1908 issue of the *Indiana Farmer*. In the photo below, Steele is standing in the back row second from the right. Isaac McNamee might be the man with the white beard standing next to Steele in the back row at the far right. The family members (seated, left to right) are Loni Dyson, Grace Dyson, Lydia Dyson, Velma (Dyson) Crist, Carl Crist, and Clarence Dyson. A more recent view of the barn shows the name by which it is now known, the Dunwiddie barn.

ELEVATION: FROM "A ROUND BARN," *INDIANA FARMER*, SEPT. 5, 1908
BARN PHOTO: 1986 FAMILY PHOTO: 1907, PHOTOGRAPHER UNKNOWN (Courtesy Elizabeth A. Meyer, granddaughter of Loni Dyson)

➤ Demaree true-circular barn,
Parke County. Built: ca. 1904; burned
down in 1986.   PHOTO: 1986

➤ T. S. Johnson
true-circular barn,
Clinton County.
Built: 1909; roof
collapsed in 1987.
PHOTO: 1986

➤ Martin L. Hofherr
true-circular barn, Dela-
ware County. Built: 1904.
PHOTO: 1986

➤ George Rudicel
12-sided barn, Shelby
County. Built: 1910.
PHOTO: 1985

◄ Edwin Mark true-
circular barn, Grant County.
Built: 1915; rebuilt in 1936
after a fire destroyed the
original barn. PHOTO: 1986

◄ Frank Dunham true-circular barn, Hancock County. Built: 1910; destroyed by windstorm in 1988.   PHOTO: 1985

V James Young, Sr., and James Clark true-circular barn, LaPorte County. Built: 1917–18; rebuilt in 1921 after a fire destroyed the original barn. PHOTO: 1986

◄ Robert F. Thompson
true-circular barn, Parke County.
Built: 1895. PHOTO: 1986

➤ Ellis and Ralph
Smith 16-sided barn,
Noble County. Built:
1911. PHOTO: 1985

A Strauther Pleak true-circular barn, Decatur County.
Built: 1911. PHOTO: 1986

≺ Oliver Perry
Watson 14-sided barn,
Huntington County.
Built: 1907–08.
PHOTO: 1986

➢ Cullen true-circular
barn, Rush County. Built:
date unknown.   PHOTO: 1985

⋏ Morton Friend
true-circular barn,
Steuben County.
Built: 1914.
Photo: 1985

⊰ Allen "Duck" Spencer true-circular barn, Clinton
County. Built: 1910.   Photo: 1986

Starbuck true-circular barn, Randolph County.
Built: pre-1905; roof collapsed in 1990.   PHOTO: 1985

William Fisher 10-sided barn, Montgomery County. Built: 1914.
PHOTO: 1986

John Holland true-circular barn, Union County. Built: 1907. PHOTO: 1985

A Wilbur Breeks 14-sided barn,
Montgomery County. Built: 1912–13.
PHOTO: 1986

➤ Henry Kemp true-circular barn, Madison County. Built: ca. 1898; dismantled in 1989. PHOTO: 1986

Preservation of the Round Barn

Indiana has been slow to recognize the historical and aesthetic value of its round barns, and preservation efforts for these structures were virtually nonexistent for years. This is unfortunate because these barns played an important role in the state's agricultural growth and experimentation to improve farming practices. Today many barns—round and rectangular—are taken for granted and are destroyed every year. Consequently, Indiana is losing an important part of its heritage. Of the 226 round barns identified in Indiana, only 111 remained as of 1992. Since 1960, roughly 40 percent, or about 88, have been destroyed for one reason or another. And this trend is continuing. A visit to four round barns near Indianapolis found that three had lost their roofs during the winter of 1987–88, and the other was completely destroyed.

It is not surprising how quickly circular barns are vanishing, since the burden of upkeep

➤ View of the T. S. Johnson barn, Clinton County. PHOTO: 1986

Λ Same view of Johnson's barn two years later. After years of neglect, the roof of the barn finally collapsed. Most of Indiana's remaining round barns will meet a similar fate if no efforts are made to fix them up.   PHOTO: 1988

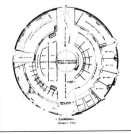

≺ This diagram shows Benton Steele's original design—probably his most complex true-circular plan ever—for the T. S. Johnson barn. Just after it was built, a photo of the barn appeared in the University of Illinois bulletin *Economy of the Round Dairy Barn.*
ELEVATION AND BARN PLAN: FROM BENTON STEELE, "THE ROUND BARN," INDIANA FARMER, NOV. 30, 1907

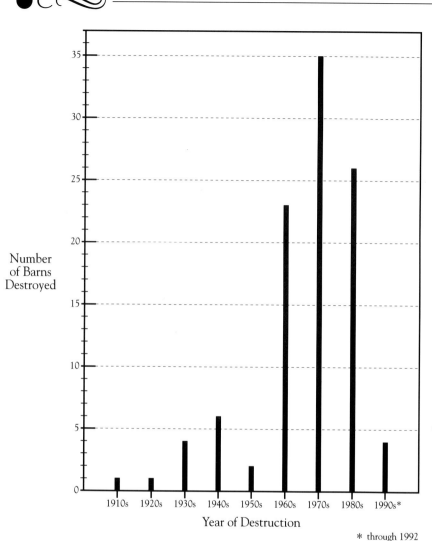

35

30

25

20

Number
of Barns
Destroyed

15

10

5

0

1910s 1920s 1930s 1940s 1950s 1960s 1970s 1980s 1990s*

Year of Destruction

* through 1992

FIGURE 4
Destruction of Round Barns in Indiana
The destruction of Indiana's round barns has accelerated in recent years. Nearly
40 percent of all barns built in the state have been destroyed since 1960. With aging
barns and exorbitant restoration costs, the trend is likely to continue unless a concerted
effort is made to save these historic structures.

Barns not represented: 13 whose destruction dates are unknown.

A View of the
Jasper Hufty barn
after it was built in
1911. PHOTO: CA.
1912, PHOTOGRAPHER
UNKNOWN (Courtesy
Everett Gruber,
grandson of
Jasper Hufty)

is generally on the shoulders of the owner, who, for the most part, cannot justify the maintenance expense. Most barns are not in use, and if tornadoes or fires do not destroy them, the lack of upkeep certainly will. More often than not, an owner will let a barn fall into disrepair. Generally, the roof goes first because over the years it loses shingles and water leaks develop. When these leaks are neglected, water seeps in and begins to rot the purlin plates and other supportive structures. As the plates rot, the roof weakens and sags. Eventually, a section collapses, then the whole roof. Once the roof falls in, it is generally too late to save the barn.

What does it cost to reshingle a roof? One that may have cost $100 to shingle in 1910 may cost $20,000 to $40,000 to reshingle today. The number of shingles involved is staggering. A 60-foot-diameter barn may require 100,000 wood shingles. A 100-foot-diameter barn may require

◄ When the Jasper Hufty round barn in Carroll County lost its roof during a tornado in 1948, members of the Purdue University Agricultural Engineering Department designed an unusual rectangular replacement. PHOTO: 1986

build a rectangular-shaped roof on top of the circular base. This unusual structure still stands today and is a landmark in the area. Jasper Hufty and the current owner, his grandson-in-law, Everett Gruber, are two of many owners with a strong sense of family pride and history with the funds to maintain their barn.

Recent years have brought other preservation efforts. In 1991, the Frank Aker, Sr., round barn located in Marshall County was moved to Amish Acres in Nappanee, Indiana, and is now used as a theater. In another attempt, the owner of the William Malott round barn in Hamilton County was willing to give the barn away to anyone who would move it, restore it, and preserve it. However, the barn burned down in 1991 before a taker was found.

The Fulton County Historical Society has undertaken the most energetic and successful salvation of a round barn to date. On September 1, 1989, a tornado blew the roof off of the Bert Leedy round barn (known locally as the Paxton round barn) in Fulton County. The Paxtons wanted to preserve it but could not afford to restore it, so they decided to donate it to the historical society. Recognizing the opportunity to save a round barn, the organization accepted the challenge to relocate it next to the Fulton County Museum. A building permit was requested and granted, and

170,000 shingles. Justifying the expenditure is difficult when the barn is no longer in use and is considered to be a relic. Given the extreme costs, most owners have found a cheaper alternative to fixing their roofs. Instead of wood shingles, they use asphalt shingles at a cost ranging from $10,000 to $20,000, which is still an extreme expense.

Some owners, however, have been able to save their barns after the loss of a roof. One particularly unusual case involved the Jasper J. Hufty barn in Carroll County. In 1948, a tornado claimed the roof of this barn. No contractor would bid on its reconstruction, so members of the Purdue University Engineering Department drew up plans to

➤ Although round barns are being destroyed every year, some owners have found unique ways to preserve their barns. This barn, built in 1916 for Lulu Swartz of Hancock County, was restored between 1985 and 1987 and converted into a beautiful house. PHOTO: 1988

funds totaling approximately $60,000, including a $40,000 short-term loan from the Historic Landmarks Foundation of Indiana, were raised to save the barn. The barn was moved during 1989 and 1990 and was opened to the public in 1991, helping Fulton County preserve its claim as the Round Barn Capital of the World.

Still other efforts are continuing. In 1991 and 1992, the author worked closely with the Historic Landmarks Foundation to catalog and document the remaining round barns in the state with the goal of identifying twenty-five to thirty worthy candidates for registration with the National Historic Register in Washington, D.C. This will allow the current owners to apply for and obtain federal financial assistance for the upkeep of these fine structures.

Finally, a plan is underway to replicate Indiana's largest round barn, the Frank Littleton

barn of Hancock County, at the Indiana State Fairgrounds in Indianapolis as part of a Hoosier farm museum complex. The project, promoted by Maurice L. Williamson, longtime manager of the Pioneer Museum at the Indiana State Fair and, former executive secretary of the Purdue University Agricultural Alumni Association will allow visitors to view turn-of-the-century farming methods and rural lifestyles and inspect the latest in agricultural advances when it is constructed. Plans call for a greenhouse, an orchard, a farm pond, and several acres of fields planted with grains and vegetables. The complex would also include a restaurant, theater, and conference center designed after a large Hamilton County cattle barn. The cost of the project is anticipated in the millions of dollars, and funding will be sought from foundations, the state, food companies, and farmers over the next few years.

Congratulations are due to these people for their involvement in preserving a part of Indiana's disappearing agricultural past. Preservation of these structures is important because the round barn has a certain charm not found outside the United States and Canada. Often seen as a lonely outpost along a quiet country road, it is the round barn, and not its rectangular counterpart, that is most remembered by rural travelers. Its perfect shape and the graceful outline are readily noticeable and visually pleasing. Travelers often stop and photograph these unique structures only to leave quickly in search of another one. In short, the round barn is a masterpiece. I hope this book will leave the reader with a greater understanding of Indiana's agricultural history and thus help delay the demise of these beautiful structures so future generations can enjoy them as I did.

Catalog of Round Barns

T he following catalog describes all 226 barns I discovered during my survey of Indiana's round barns. Of these, only 111 were still standing in 1992. Included is a summary of what I've learned about each barn's history with specific references, if known, to the locations, construction dates, original owners, architects, and builders. If available, a representative photograph of each barn is also included. The photo credit line indicates the date of the photograph and gives the name of the photographer if it was someone other than myself.

With the variety of sources I consulted, it was not uncommon to find incomplete information and contradictions of facts.[1] I attempted to sift through these discrepancies and determine the most accurate or plausible data. I consider the information in this catalog to be the most accurate compiled to date. Additional research, however, is likely to reveal more inaccuracies or omissions that should be brought to my attention.

I've assigned a two-part code to every barn in the catalog. The first two digits correspond with the alpha-numeric sequence for the county. For instance, Indiana has ninety-two counties. Alphabetically, Adams County is the first, so it is 01; Allen County is the second, 02; and Whitley County is the last, 92. The number following the dash corresponds with the number of barns found in the county. A "1" would be the first barn counted; a "2," the second; and so on. This numbering system is similar to that used by Gene Worl. Twenty counties are not listed because no round barns were found in those counties.

John T. Hanou

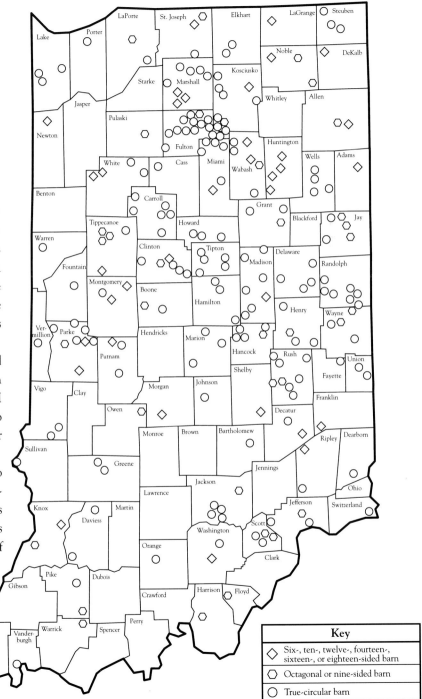

Key	
◇	Six-, ten-, twelve-, fourteen-, sixteen-, or eighteen-sided barn
⬡	Octagonal or nine-sided barn
○	True-circular barn

Adams County

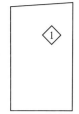

01-1: SIX-SIDED BARN

BUILT: ca. 1907
SITE: St. Mary's Township
ORIGINAL OWNER: Ben Colter
BUILDER: Ben Colter
PHOTO: 1985

One of three 6-sided barns identified in Indiana, this barn was constructed by Ben Colter, who was a banker, schoolteacher, and sawmill operator. The sides were constructed flat on the ground, then hoisted into place using a central post. Horses were kept on the south side, cattle on the east, and sheep on the north. The west side was used for storage. The central wood silo is held together by metal compression rings. A sectional cone roof and a six-sided cupola top the barn. A rectangular attachment was added later for raising hogs.

Allen County

02-1: TWELVE-SIDED BARN

BUILT: ca. 1908 (razed, 1960s)
SITE: Adams Township
ORIGINAL OWNER: W. D. Holterman
ARCHITECT/BUILDER: unknown
PHOTO: From "Ten Thousand Dollars a Year from Barred Rocks," *Farmer's Guide*, Mar. 20, 1915

The following is an excerpt from a 1915 issue of the *Farmer's Guide:* "W. D. Holterman was an entrepreneur from the start. In 1900 he worked as a small salaried clerk in Fort Wayne. To make both ends meet he decided to raise poultry as a sideline. He realized that the most money to be made would be from purebred high class birds, such as Barred Plymouth Rock chickens. After eight years, he quit his job and expanded his business by buying seven acres of land east of the city. Here he built several buildings, including his residence, constructed of stone, and the large twelve-sided chicken house. He was quite successful, as indicated by his gross sales which averaged $10,000 in 1915. The chicken house was a two storied breeding pen. It contains eleven pens downstairs, with over 120 square feet of floor space, and eleven conditioning pens upstairs, each containing 40 square feet of floor space. The feed room, containing 225 square feet of floor space, is in the center of the building under the dome. The eleven pens radiate out from this central feed room like spokes of a wheel.... All ventilation is out through the windows in the dome. Mr. Holterman says this type of house is the most economical and convenient he has ever used or seen."

02-2: OCTAGONAL BARN

BUILT: date unknown (destroyed, date unknown)
SITE: Adams Township
ORIGINAL OWNER: unknown
ARCHITECT/BUILDER: unknown
PHOTO: 1969, Gene Worl

Nothing is known about this barn except that it was probably located in Allen County east of Fort Wayne on U.S. Highway 30. There is a strong possibility that it stood on the W. D. Holterman farm.

Bartholomew County

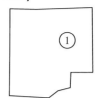

03-1: TRUE-CIRCULAR BARN

BUILT: ca. 1903 (razed, 1974)
SITE: Clifty Township
ORIGINAL OWNER: Edward May
ARCHITECTS/BUILDERS: probably Emery and Isaac McNamee and Benton Steele
PHOTO: ca. 1930, photographer unknown (Courtesy Dorothy Evans)

Bartholomew County's only round barn was razed in 1974 to make room for the widening of State Road 9. Efforts to save the barn failed when only a few thousand of the required $80,000 to move the barn was raised. It closely resembled a McNamee barn built in Fayette County in 1904, thus McNamee probably constructed this one. This barn had an interesting combination of concrete-block and horizontal and vertical siding. Additional information on this barn can be found in Sam Parker, "Round Barn May Be Around," *Columbus* (Ind.) *Republic Week Ender*, Feb. 10, 1973, 1.

Boone County

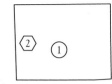

06-1: TRUE-CIRCULAR BARN

BUILT: 1912–13
SITE: Center Township
ORIGINAL OWNER: Andrew B. Van Huys
BUILDER: Andrew B. Van Huys
PHOTO: 1969, Gene Worl

This barn is one of four concrete-block round barns identified in Indiana. It is 50 feet in diameter with a 17-foot wall that encloses approximately 2,000 square feet of floor space. A four-windowed cupola that topped the self-supporting roof no longer exists. The roof, originally covered with slate, is now covered with asbestos shingles and requires the support of eight interior posts. A north-south driveway passes through the barn. For more information, see Ralph W. Stark, "No Corners Found in Barn That's Round," *Boone: Your County Magazine*, vol. 1, no. 4 (May 1974), 10.

06-2: Octagonal barn

Built: 1894

Site: Jefferson Township

Original owner: David W. Reed, Sr.

Builder: David W. Reed, Sr.

Photo: 1986

Measuring 50 feet in diameter with north-south entries, this is the first circular silo barn built in Indiana. Extending to and supporting the roof, the central wood-stave silo is held together by metal compression rings and can be filled through the small gable-roofed dormer located on the south side of the barn's roof.

Carroll County

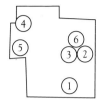

08-1: True-circular barn

Built: 1912

Site: Democrat Township

Original owner: Albert Aikens

Builder: Albert Aikens

Photo: 1960, George Gould

When Aikens built this barn, he used the first vertical timber as a pattern for cutting the second one, and the second as a pattern for the third, and so on. Consequently, the final upright was a foot shorter than the first, and the end result was a roof that leaned a little. The barn is 50 feet in diameter with two north-south entries and a two-pitch gambrel roof. A circular hay track is present inside. Originally used as a horse sale barn, it was altered to a milk house in 1950. Today it shelters hogs. In 1918, an Indianapolis man, believed to be Horace Duncan, contacted Aikens claiming patent ownership to the barn. Threatened with legal action, Aikens decided to pay the $85 fee for the right to the patent.

08-2: True-circular barn

Built: 1915

Site: Carrollton Township

Original owner: Smiley

Architects/Builders: C.V. Kindig and Sons

Photo: 1987

This barn is believed to be the second round barn built for the Smiley family; the first was built in Fulton County. A large gable-roofed hay dormer provides access to the hay mow, and the two-pitch gambrel roof once supported a cupola. Built on a poured-concrete foundation, the barn has vertical wood siding and an east-west entry.

08-3: True-circular barn

Built: 1910

Site: Jackson Township

Original owner: unknown

Architect/Builder: unknown

Photo: 1985

This barn originally had a cupola, but it was destroyed many years ago. A glazed-tile silo is located near the southwest side of the barn, and an east-west driveway passes through the barn.

08-4: True-circular barn

Built: 1904 (destroyed by fire, 1978)

Site: Jefferson Township

Original owner: David Lilly

Architect: probably Benton Steele

Builders: Aaron Breckbill, Jesse Viney, Andy Fisher, and Joe Denton

Photo: 1960, George Gould

Located on the Linden-Vale farm, the framing for this 51-foot-diameter barn came from linden and elm trees, which were cut on the farm. The siding was pine. A 12-foot-diameter silo located in the center was 35 feet tall. Access to the second floor was provided by a ramp. Head carpenter Aaron Breckbill of Burnettsville, was assisted by Jesse Viney of Yeoman and Andy Fisher of Monticello. Joe Denton put up the stone foundation. The Linden-Vale barn closely resembled some of Benton Steele's designs advertised in the *Indiana Farmer*.

08-5: True-circular barn

Built: 1911–12

Site: Tippecanoe Township

Original owner: Jasper J. Hufty

Architect: Horace Duncan

Builder: Charles Baker

Photo: 1986

The following is excerpted from Wilson Wells's *Barns in the U.S.A.:* "When Jasper J. Hufty stood in front of his new barn in 1911 he was pleased with what he saw. The original color was orange with white trim.... Large stalls were built around the outside, facing toward the center and with a circular feeding alley at the horses' heads. [A] complete circular hay track ran around the loft so hay could be drawn up from the wagon at either end of the driveway. Oak sawed on the farm was used for the heavy beams. When the original roof was blown off in a tornado in 1948, no contractor would bid on reconstruction." Eventually, members of the Purdue University Agricultural Engineering Department drew up plans to repair the roof. Instead of a circular roof, they designed and built a rectangular one in 1951. The original roof was a two-pitch gambrel roof with a cupola on top.

08-6: *TRUE-CIRCULAR BARN*

BUILT: date unknown
(razed, 1950s)
SITE: Washington Township
ORIGINAL OWNER: Isaac Wolfe
ARCHITECT/BUILDER: unknown
PHOTO: not available

Little is known about this barn except that Isaac Wolfe was an uncle of Truman Planck, the current owner of barn #08-1 in Carroll County. Wolfe's barn was built on a bank with the lower entry facing south. The lower level had poured-concrete walls, and a single hay track was located inside the barn.

Cass County

09-1: *TRUE-CIRCULAR BARN*

BUILT: date unknown
(destroyed, 1960s)
SITE: Boone Township
ORIGINAL OWNER: Roy Brown
ARCHITECT/BUILDER: unknown
PHOTO: not available

A circular barn was once located on the Roy Brown farm a half mile north of Royal Center. No other information is available on the history of this barn.

Clinton County

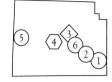

12-1: *TRUE-CIRCULAR BARN*

BUILT: 1910
SITE: Sugar Creek Township
ORIGINAL OWNER:
Allen "Duck" Spencer
BUILDER: Melvin Johnson
PHOTO: 1986

One of three or possibly four round barns built by the Johnson family of Kempton, this one is 60 feet in diameter with a 10-foot-wide, east-west driveway through the middle. A round corn crib is on the north side near horse stalls and feed bunkers. The walls were originally constructed with horizontal wood siding from the ground to the roof; however, the lower portion of the siding rotted out and was replaced with concrete blocks. The barn has a 12-foot-diameter cupola and a two-pitch gambrel roof. A granary used to be in the hay mow, but it was removed years ago. Additional information on this barn can be found in Kathy Slaughter, "Well-rounded Barn Helps To Cut Corners," *Frankfort Times*, Oct. 14, 1985.

12-2: *TRUE-CIRCULAR BARN*

BUILT: 1909
(roof collapsed, 1987)
SITE: Kirklin Township
ORIGINAL OWNER:
T. S. Johnson
ARCHITECT/BUILDER:
Benton Steele
PHOTO: 1986

This truly magnificent barn is one of a kind. It had a monitor roof requiring support and an unusual gable-roofed entrance. A north-south driveway passes through the barn. Concrete blocks and round windows and vents give the barn its character. The barn is 90 feet in diameter, making it one of the largest in Indiana. A concrete silo was once located on the west side of the barn. The future of this barn is uncertain; the top portion of roof collapsed in 1987. A plan and description of a smaller version of this barn were described by Benton Steele in "The Round Barn," *Indiana Farmer*, Nov. 30, 1907, 1. A photograph of this barn appeared in the University of Illinois bulletin *Economy of the Round Dairy Barn*.

12-3: *TWELVE-SIDED BARN*

BUILT: ca. 1900
SITE: Michigan Township
ORIGINAL OWNER: unknown
ARCHITECT/BUILDER: unknown
PHOTO: 1986

This attractive barn has a sectional-cone, two-pitch roof that requires posts for support. Instead of a cupola, there are four dormers. The barn has a north-south driveway through the center.

12-4: *OCTAGONAL BARN*

BUILT: 1914–15 (razed, 1983)
SITE: Union Township
ORIGINAL OWNER:
Elmer or D. C. Slipher
ARCHITECT/BUILDER:
Elmer or D. C. Slipher
PHOTO: ca. 1970, Harry Sheets
(Courtesy Mrs. Harry Sheets)

Built as a bank barn and used for dairy purposes, the Slipher barn had 22 cattle stanchions surrounding a feed bin in the center of the lower level. An underground subwalk provided access to a large rectangular barn to the south. Entry to the second level of the octagonal barn consisted of a long rectangular structure topped with a two-pitch gambrel roof. Under the driveway there was a milk cooling room and a motorized milking machine. The barn had a sectional, two-pitch gambrel roof and an octagonal cupola. A photograph of the interior appeared in the September 15, 1917, issue of the *Farmer's Guide*.

12-5: *TRUE-CIRCULAR BARN*

BUILT: 1912
SITE: Madison Township
ORIGINAL OWNER:
J. Seymour Clendenning
BUILDER: A. Meyers
PHOTO: 1986

This barn gained some popularity in "A Big Round Barn," *Farmer's Guide*, Sept. 6, 1913, 5: "The barn is 66 feet in diameter and its height in the center to the top of the cupola is 70 feet. In the center is a silo 12 by 49 feet, the first nine feet being in the basement. The basement wall is ten feet high and from the top of the wall to the eaves is 18 feet. The entrance to the main floor [faces] west and there is a driveway around the silo. A load of hay can be

driven in, around the silo and out again at the same place if it is desired. On the north side are the horse stalls, the horses facing the driveway. On the south side is a large mow and there is also a mow over the horses. Above is a circular track extending the whole distance around so that hay or other forage can be unloaded wherever it is wanted. . . . The basement extends under about half the barn. In one apartment are stalls for five cows and the rest is all in one enclosure in which steers are fed. The floor of this apartment is of cement and there are racks and feeders into which the feed comes from the next floor. The east side of this room is open, the cattle fed there furnishing plenty of warmth to keep themselves comfortable in the coldest winter weather."

12-6: *TRUE-CIRCULAR BARN*

BUILT: pre-1911
(destroyed, ca. 1960)
SITE: Michigan Township
ORIGINAL OWNER: Goff
ARCHITECT/BUILDER:
probably Melvin Johnson
PHOTO: not available

Little is known about this barn except that it was probably built by Melvin Johnson, who also built three other barns in the vicinity. It was located about a mile west of Hillisburg on the north side of the railroad tracks. A silo once stood next to barn.

Daviess County

14-1: *TRUE-CIRCULAR BARN*

BUILT: 1908
SITE: Veale Township
ORIGINAL OWNER:
Thomas C. Singleton
ARCHITECT: Benton Steele
BUILDERS: Bugler, G. Scudder, and A. Ragsdale
PHOTO: 1985

Thomas Singleton described his barn in the June 5, 1909, issue of the *Indiana Farmer*: "This barn is sixty four (64) feet in diameter and eighteen (18) feet to the eaves. A driveway passes through the center of the barn and is also arranged to drive around behind the stock in hauling out manure, etc. One half can be used for cattle or loose stock of any kind or for vehicles and machinery, if desired. The feeding is all done from the center of the barn. Bins are arranged on either side of the driveway for holding of grain and a corn crib four and one-

half feet wide (4½) extends around [a quarter] the distance of the barn. The hay is taken up from the driveway just inside the large door by means of a circular haying outfit. The roof of the barn is entirely self-supporting, there being no timbers to obstruct the mow place. After using this barn for several months I have no hesitancy in recommending the 'Circular Barn' as the most convenient and most practical barn for farmers and stockmen."

14-2: *TRUE-CIRCULAR BARN*

BUILT: early 1900s
SITE: Elmore Township
ORIGINAL OWNER: Charles Sims
BUILDER: Charles Sims
PHOTO: 1985

Huge logs for timbers in the base, studding, and rafters of this barn came from the farm where it is located. One large door with perfect symmetry is accented by roofing over the entrance, which allows the farmer to drive fully loaded hay racks into the barn for unloading. There is a north-south driveway through the center. Metal sheeting covers half of the roof.

Dearborn County

15-1: *TRUE-CIRCULAR BARN*

BUILT: 1901–02
SITE: Clay Township
ORIGINAL OWNER:
Wymond J. Beckett
ARCHITECT/BUILDER:
Benton Steele
PHOTO: 1978, George Gould

This is one of two circular barns built for Congressman Beckett, and one of the first designed by Benton Steele. At 100 feet in diameter, it was the largest in the state at the time it was built. As a bank barn, it had a ramp to the second floor and a 16-foot-diameter windmill extending through the roof. The windmill only lasted a short time before it was destroyed by high winds. Large wooden storage tanks located on the hay mow floor were used to provide running water for the 800-acre farm. The domed roof is only one of three built in Indiana. Four posts support the

roof. The construction brought considerable fame to Steele and Beckett, and it prompted the construction of the 102-foot-diameter masterpiece on the Frank Littleton farm in Hancock County. A photograph and story of this barn appeared in the December 22, 1906, issue of the *Indiana Farmer*, and Steele later described it in *Farm Buildings*, published by *Breeder's Gazette* in 1913. The cupola shown in the photograph no longer exists. The entire barn was remodeled in 1964, when concrete and masonite were added for appearance and durability.

Decatur County

16-1: *TRUE-CIRCULAR BARN*

BUILT: 1911
SITE: Washington Township
ORIGINAL OWNER: Strauther Pleak
BUILDER: Strauther Pleak
PHOTO: 1986

Resembling a three-tier wedding cake, the Pleak round barn is one of the most aesthetically pleasing in Indiana. It also features an octagonal silo in the center, a double cupola, and horizontal siding. The 18-foot-diameter silo, lined with brick and concrete, was constructed first; and the barn was erected around it. The conical roof is supported by the silo. A large rectangular addition is attached to the north side of the barn.

16-2: *FOURTEEN-SIDED BARN*

BUILT: 1913
(destroyed by tornado, 1974)
SITE: Salt Creek Township
ORIGINAL OWNER: William Cramer
ARCHITECT: probably Chicago Wrecking House Co.
BUILDERS: Frank Nedderman and Bill Dickman
PHOTO: 1970, Gene Worl

This is one of two 14-sided barns designed and built by Nedderman, a contractor from Batesville. Nedderman probably obtained the idea from the Chicago Wrecking House Company, which periodically advertised similar plans in issues of the *Indiana Farmer* and the *Breeder's Gazette*. Cramer's barn stood 56 feet high and 60 feet in diameter, and had a north-south driveway. It could hold nine horses, 10 beef cows, and 10 milk cows. Over 120 tons of hay could be stored in the loft.

DeKalb County

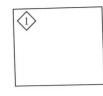

17-1: *FOURTEEN-SIDED BARN*

BUILT: 1910
SITE: Fairfield Township
ORIGINAL OWNERS: Maria and Franklin Wiltrout
ARCHITECT: probably Chicago Wrecking House Co.
BUILDER: Frank Reynolds
PHOTO: 1985

Reports are that plans for this barn were obtained through a Montgomery Ward or Sears catalog; however, except for lacking a silo in the center, this barn appears to be a duplicate of "Round Barn Design No. 206" as advertised by the Chicago Wrecking House Company in the *Indiana Farmer* in 1910. It has 14 sides, each 14 feet long. It can hold 160 tons of hay and accommodate 100 head of cattle. All materials were probably precut and delivered by the Chicago Wrecking House Company. Excluding delivery, the materials probably cost less than $1,000.

Delaware County

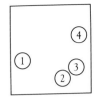

18-1: *TRUE-CIRCULAR BARN*

BUILT: 1904
SITE: Mt. Pleasant Township
ORIGINAL OWNER: Martin L. Hofherr
ARCHITECTS/BUILDERS: probably Benton Steele, Isaac and Emery McNamee, and Horace Duncan
PHOTO: 1987

The roof of this barn closely resembles one designed and built by Steele, Duncan, and the McNamees for F. W. Boettcher near Artis, South Dakota. Since these builders were in the Delaware County area of Indiana in 1904, they probably designed and constructed the Hofherr barn. An old photograph supports this claim because it appears that Duncan is posed in the front of the barn with the owner. Constructed as a draft horse barn, it was built on the side of a bank on a stone foundation. It is 72 feet high and 70 feet in diameter. There are four entries and numerous windows.

It is described by the present owner, Philip M. Hofherr, in Wilson Wells's *Barns in the U.S.A.*: "There are 12 stalls in half of the exposed circumference of the lower wall, two grain bins and two box stalls with an inner circle walkway with crosswalk in the center. The floor of the hayloft is made of 1x2-inch and 2x2-inch wood boards laid on edge in a circular pattern from the outside perimeter for approximately 20 feet toward the center of the barn. The wood was water soaked so as to curve correctly and nailed into place." Martin L. Hofherr was a son of Philip Hofherr, who was concertmaster to Swedish soprano Jenny Lind during an 1850–52 American tour.

18-2: TRUE-CIRCULAR BARN

BUILT: 1908
SITE: Perry Township
ORIGINAL OWNER: Albert Leroy Keesling
ARCHITECT: Benton Steele
BUILDER: Horace Duncan
PHOTO: 1985

The first of two round barns built for Keesling is 52 feet in diameter with horizontal wood siding, a silo in the center, and an unusual octagonal cupola. Both of the Keesling barns have a unique floor plan that was pre-

sented by Benton Steele in "Two Barns Compared," *Indiana Farmer*, Dec. 15, 1906. Most circular silo barns do not have enough room for a driveway to pass through them; however, in this variation, entry doors were constructed in such a way to allow the farmer to pull a wagon through the barn, skirting the side of the silo and still allowing easy access to it. The design also provided an excellent place for storing equipment.

18-3: TRUE-CIRCULAR BARN

BUILT: ca. 1909
SITE: Liberty Township
ORIGINAL OWNER: Albert Leroy Keesling
ARCHITECT: Benton Steele
PHOTO: 1968, Gene Worl

The second Keesling barn is almost identical to the first except this one measures 48 feet across instead of 52 feet. Each barn has a poured-concrete foundation extending two to three feet above the ground, and each has a two-pitch gambrel roof. The barns were originally used for dairy purposes.

18-4: TRUE-CIRCULAR BARN

BUILT: 1908
SITE: Delaware Township
ORIGINAL OWNER: Cirus Stafford
ARCHITECT/BUILDER: probably Benton Steele
PHOTO: 1985

At 80 feet in diameter and 75 feet high, the roof of this barn requires support of a derrick-like structure, which extends from the hay mow to the cupola. It was probably designed by Benton Steele, since it closely resembles a barn described by him in "A Circular Barn with Silo," *Breeder's Gazette*, July 2, 1902, 43–45.

Elkhart County

20-1: TRUE-CIRCULAR BARN

BUILT: ca. 1908 (destroyed by fire, 1977)
SITE: Harrison Township
ORIGINAL OWNER: Erias Snyder
ARCHITECT: probably Benton Steele
BUILDER: Philip Lauderman
PHOTO: From "Round Barns," *Indiana Farmer*, May 14, 1910

Snyder's barn was one of at least four round barns built by Philip Lauderman of Breman. Benton Steele was probably the architect because he designed and built Moses Whitehead's barn (#20-2) nearby at about the same time. The Snyder barn was described in typical Steele fashion in a 1910 *Indiana Farmer* article: "This barn is 60 feet in diameter, 24 feet siding, and 54 feet to the top of the cupola. It has four blinds and 26 windows. . . . The roof is self-supporting. The barn has a circular hay track in it which makes it much

more convenient to handle hay or grain with slings than in the ordinary square barn. . . . The structure will hold 100 tons of hay. Could be arranged so as to stable 15 head of horses, 30 head of cattle, 45 head in all. In fact the same room can be had at a savings of about one-fourth the material used in a square barn. The approximate cost of the barn . . . is $1,200."

20-2: TRUE-CIRCULAR BARN

BUILT: 1908 (damaged by tornado, 1936; dismantled, 1936–40)
SITE: Union Township
ORIGINAL OWNER: Moses A. Whitehead
ARCHITECT/BUILDER: Benton Steele
PHOTO: 1937, Lowell Blocker (Courtesy Ella Kaufman)

The photograph shows the barn after a tornado partially collapsed it in 1936. During the next four years it was completely dismantled. It was a bank barn with a concrete-block basement and vertical wood siding. It did not have a silo, but it had a self-supporting, three-pitch gambrel roof.

Fayette County

21-1: *TRUE-CIRCULAR BARN*

BUILT: 1904
SITE: Waterloo Township
ORIGINAL OWNERS:
Thomas and Nancy Ranck
ARCHITECT/BUILDER:
Isaac McNamee
PHOTO: 1985

Isaac McNamee built this barn in 1904. His son Emery rebuilt the roof in the early 1930s after a tornado tore off the old roof. Emery was in his early eighties at the time and, according to some sources, made quite a bit of money on it because he was the only contractor who knew how to fix it. From the exterior, this barn appears to have three tiers, but the interior above the hay mow (second floor) is all open. At least two other circular barns in Indiana resemble this plan. An earthen ramp provides access to the hay mow, and the large horse-drawn hayforks with ropes and pulleys for unloading loose hay are still in place. Originally used for livestock, it now houses Chester White hogs. A concrete floor in the lower level provides an excellent feeding base for the livestock. The barn, known locally as the McDivitt round barn, is listed with the Historic American Building Survey. Benton Steele may have designed this one because it resembles one advertised by him in the *Indiana Farmer*.

Floyd County

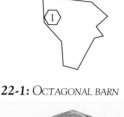

22-1: *OCTAGONAL BARN*

BUILT: date unknown
(razed, 1970s)
SITE: Greenville Township
ORIGINAL OWNER: unknown
ARCHITECT/BUILDER: unknown
PHOTO: 1970, Gene Worl

Very little is known about this structure. It was a bank barn that was probably used for hogs. The sectional cone roof did not have a cupola.

Fountain County

23-1: *TRUE-CIRCULAR BARN*

BUILT: 1907 (razed, 1989)
SITE: Richland Township
ORIGINAL OWNER:
Edward Death
ARCHITECT/BUILDER: unknown
PHOTO: ca. 1960,
George Gould

This was the only Indiana circular barn constructed entirely with brick. Each brick measured 4x4x8 inches and had the inscription "W. F. Co. Culver Block Pat. May 11, 1901." The barn measured 60 feet across with a north-south driveway. Inside the 20-foot-diameter cupola there was a wheel that could be turned to open and close the cupola windows. The barn had a self-supporting conical roof with a single hay track.

Franklin County

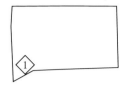

24-1: *FOURTEEN-SIDED BARN*

BUILT: 1915
(destroyed by fire, 1957)
SITE: Ray Township
ORIGINAL OWNER:
Robert Koester
ARCHITECT:
Frank H. Nedderman
BUILDER: Bill Dickman
PHOTO: date and
photographer unknown
(Courtesy Zane Koester)

Relatives of the original owner provided the following history for this barn: It was one of two round barns built by Frank Nedderman of Batesville. It was also one of three round barns in Indiana with the original set of blueprints still in existence. The barn measured 60 feet across. The sides were 13$\frac{1}{2}$ feet long each. Of the fourteen sides, 12 had a small door for access into each stall. The other two sides had large sliding doors. Horse stalls were located on one side, and cattle stalls on the other. Twelve mangers surrounded the 12-foot-diameter silo. The self-supporting, two-pitch sectional roof was topped with an eight-sided cupola.

Fulton County

25-1: TRUE-CIRCULAR BARN

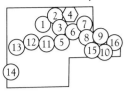

BUILT: 1924 (lost roof, 1989; relocated and restored, 1990)
SITE: Richland Township
ORIGINAL OWNER: Bert Leedy
ARCHITECTS/BUILDERS: C.V. Kindig and Sons
PHOTO: 1985

Bert Leedy's barn was the last to be built by the Kindig builders. As a bank barn, it measures 60 feet across and has a three-pitch gambrel roof. Doris Hood wrote in *Fulton County's Round Barns:* "The barn originally was used to house farm animals. For many years the lower level sheltered as many as eight horses, 30 sheep, eight cows, eight calves, and eight feeding steers. After harvest time the top of the barn would be filled with 50 or 60 loads of hay and 10 to 12 loads of straw for bedding. There was a wheat bin which held 230 bushels of grain or feed." In 1989, a tornado blew off the barn's roof. The Fulton County Historical Society raised the necessary funds to move and rebuild the barn next to the his-

torical museum on U.S. 31 north of Rochester. The barn was opened to the public in 1991.

25-2: TRUE-CIRCULAR BARN

BUILT: 1917 (razed, 1977)
SITE: Richland Township
ORIGINAL OWNER: Ezra Leedy
ARCHITECTS/BUILDERS: C.V. Kindig and Sons
PHOTO: 1971, George Gould

Built by the Kindigs, this round barn was characterized by its unusual cupola, positioned on top of the two-pitch gambrel roof. Doris Hood wrote that a concrete-block foundation three blocks high was used on the west side and "only one high on the east, indicating that they milked on the west side when it was new."

25-3: TRUE-CIRCULAR BARN

BUILT: ca. 1915 (destroyed by fire, 1975)
SITE: Richland Township
ORIGINAL OWNER: Billy Strouderman

ARCHITECTS/BUILDERS: C.V. Kindig and Sons
PHOTO: 1970, Gene Worl

This 60-foot-diameter dairy barn had a concrete foundation, a central driveway, and a two-pitch gambrel roof. A small metal aerator topped the building. This barn was one of ten round barns that the Kindigs built in the county.

25-4: NINE-SIDED BARN

BUILT: pre-1921
SITE: Newcastle Township
ORIGINAL OWNER: John W. Mikesell
ARCHITECTS/BUILDERS: C.V. Kindig and Sons
PHOTO: 1985

"The barn was built by the Kindigs previous to 1921 and was a hog barn. The hog pens were used in the shape of a pie wedge with a cement trough at the narrow end. A heavy gate was hung over each trough. The top brace was a 2x4 whittled round at each end and was set in a U-shaped brace. This allowed the gate to swing either way so that the feed, which was mostly slop in those days, could be poured into the trough from one side and taken by hogs from

the other side. The gates would swing just enough to allow the slop to be poured and the hogs to feed." (Doris Hood, *Fulton County's Round Barns*)

25-5: TRUE-CIRCULAR BARN

BUILT: 1914
SITE: Rochester Township
ORIGINAL OWNER: John Haimbaugh
ARCHITECTS/BUILDERS: C.V. Kindig and Sons
PHOTO: 1985

This picturesque barn measures 72 feet across, not including the 20-foot-wide wing on the west side of the barn. Inside there are 38 milk-cow stanchions with a manure track around the milking area. Two silos were once attached to the barn but were removed years ago. Sycamore and elm trees were cut at the nearby Talma sawmill, and the green lumber was used to construct the barn because it was easier to bend than a hardwood. The self-supporting roof has a small metal cupola and a gable-roofed hay dormer on the north side.

25-6: TRUE-CIRCULAR BARN

BUILT: 1912 (destroyed by tornado, 1974)
SITE: Newcastle Township
ORIGINAL OWNER: Frank Montgomery
ARCHITECTS/BUILDERS: C.V. Kindig and Sons
PHOTO: 1960, George Gould

This bank barn had a three-pitch gambrel roof and a round cupola with 16 vents. The lower level walls were constructed with poured concrete, and the upper level had vertical siding. Thirty-five cows could be milked at one time, and as many as 6,000 bales of hay could be stored in the hay mow.

25-7: *TRUE-CIRCULAR BARN*

BUILT: 1911
SITE: Newcastle Township
ORIGINAL OWNER:
Frank Drudge
ARCHITECT/BUILDER: unknown
PHOTO: 1985

Frank Drudge's 63-foot-diameter barn can hold 5,000 bales of hay in the mow. It has a two-pitch gambrel roof and a poured-concrete foundation. The current owner claims that the barn is expensive to maintain because the outside doors and their tracks often need replacing due to wind and rain damage.

25-8: *TRUE-CIRCULAR BARN*

BUILT: 1918 (razed, 1975)
SITE: Newcastle Township
ORIGINAL OWNER: unknown
ARCHITECT/BUILDER:
Sam Nelson
PHOTO: 1969, Gene Worl

This half-circular barn was attached to a rectangular structure that was built in the early 1890s. It never had a cupola. Originally the barn was used to house sheep and chickens, but it was later converted to a dairy barn.

25-9: *TRUE-CIRCULAR BARN*

BUILT: 1910
SITE: Henry Township
ORIGINAL OWNERS: Henry, Jim, and Chost Wideman
ARCHITECTS/BUILDERS:
C.V. Kindig and Sons
PHOTO: 1985

Metal cupolas are uncommon in Indiana. Three of the sixteen circular barns built in Fulton County have them as replacements for the original wood-and-glass cupolas. This one measures about eight feet across and five feet high. The barn, measuring 70 feet across, has a central driveway and a two-pitch, self-supporting gambrel roof. The interior features a silo off to one side. Two grain bins and a corn crib surround the silo. Now used for storage, the barn originally housed cattle, pigs, and horses.

25-10: *TRUE-CIRCULAR BARN*

BUILT: 1910
SITE: Henry Township
ORIGINAL OWNER:
Elmer Wideman
ARCHITECTS/BUILDERS:
C.V. Kindig and Sons
PHOTO: 1985

This was the first round barn built in Fulton County and the first of two round barns built on the Wideman brothers' farms. It measures 60 feet across with a north-south driveway through the center. A metal cupola replaces the original wood-and-glass cupola at the top of the two-pitch gambrel roof. A silo was once located on the west side. The barn is still used as it was originally: to shelter cattle.

25-11: *TRUE-CIRCULAR BARN*

BUILT: 1912
SITE: Rochester Township
ORIGINAL OWNER: John West
ARCHITECTS/BUILDERS:
C.V. Kindig and Sons
PHOTO: 1985

At 40 feet in diameter, this is the smallest true-circular barn in Fulton County and one of the smallest in Indiana. Located on the Appaloosa Pony Farm, it has a concrete base and a two-pitch gambrel roof. The cupola began leaking and was removed in the 1950s by the barn's owner, Don Smiley.

25-12: *TRUE-CIRCULAR BARN*

BUILT: 1916
(destroyed by tornado, 1974)
SITE: Rochester Township
ORIGINAL OWNER: Zegafuse
ARCHITECTS/BUILDERS:
C.V. Kindig and Sons, and Reed Powell
PHOTO: ca. 1960, George Gould

This 72-foot-diameter barn had a concrete-block foundation and a driveway through its center. A bull pen was located on one side, and a calf pen on the other. A milking parlor and holding pen were located on the north side. The barn had windows in groups of four around its perimeter.

25-13: *TRUE-CIRCULAR BARN*

BUILT: 1910
(destroyed by tornado, 1974)
SITE: Union Township
ORIGINAL OWNER: E. B. Cook
ARCHITECT/BUILDER: unknown
PHOTO: ca. 1961,
George Gould

When this barn was built in 1910, E. B. Cook owned the farm, but William Hendrickson lived there. A bank barn, it was one of two in Fulton County with horizontal wood siding and the only one with a conical roof. The lower level, constructed with poured concrete, was used for dairy purposes. At one time there was a cupola and an exterior silo, but they were removed after a tornado damaged them in the 1950s.

25-14: *TRUE-CIRCULAR BARN*

BUILT: 1907
SITE: Wayne Township
ORIGINAL OWNER: Tom Jones
BUILDERS: Tom and Arthur Jones
PHOTO: 1986

As one of two circular barns in Fulton County with horizontal siding, this one measures 55 feet across with a silo in the center. Doris Hood wrote that Arthur "worked in a sawmill as a young man. It became necessary for him to take his wages in the form of lumber. Since the family needed a barn they decided to build. The father (Tom) wanted a regular barn but the young man insisted on trying the new novel idea—the round barn."

25-15: *True-circular barn*

Built: 1915
Site: Henry Township
Original owner: Oliver P. Utter
Builders: Hammond brothers and Courtney and Sumner Rhodes
Photo: 1985

According to Doris Hood, the carpenters stayed with the Utters during construction of this barn. It was built with lumber from the farm, which was hauled to Sayger sawmill in Akron, Indiana, for cutting. The carpenters submerged the lumber in a nearby creek to make the boards easier to bend to fit the planned structure. Measuring 69 feet across, the bank barn has a stone foundation and a three-pitch gambrel roof topped with a metal cupola. Livestock are kept in the lower level, and hay and farm equipment are stored in the upper level. Located on the Pasture Brook Farm, this attractive barn was featured on the cover of Darryl Jones's book, *Indiana* (Portland, Oreg.: Graphic Arts Center Publishing Company, 1984).

25-16: *True-circular barn*

Built: 1909–10 (destroyed by fire, 1966)
Site: Henry Township
Original owner: Albert Barnes
Architect/Builder: unknown
Photo: ca. 1960s, photographer unknown (Courtesy Roy L. Adams)

This 60-foot-diameter barn had vertical wood siding and an east-west driveway. A silo was located on the south side. Little else is known about this barn.

Grant County

27-1: *True-circular barn*

Built: 1912
Site: Van Buren Township
Original owner: Doyle
Architect/Builder: unknown
Photo: 1986

A self-supporting, two-pitch gambrel roof was built on this barn after a 1913 tornado destroyed the original domed roof. The barn is 60 feet in diameter with an east-west driveway and horizontal wood siding. It is currently used for hogs and sheep.

27-2, 27-2A: *True-circular barn*

Built: 1915 (destroyed by fire, 1935; rebuilt, 1936)
Site: Richland Township
Original owner: Edwin Mark
Architect/Builder: unknown
Photo: 1986

In 1915, Edwin Mark and his mother visited the Indiana State Fair, where they saw exhibits promoting round barns. Convinced that they should have one, too, construction on a 70-foot-diameter version started shortly after. The barn burned down in 1935, but a new barn with a larger roof was built over the same foundation in 1936. The three-pitch gambrel roof requires the support of a central hay chute that extends from the hay mow to the cupola. Metal sheeting now partially covers the sides.

27-3: *Octagonal barn*

Built: 1887
Site: Monroe Township
Original owner: John Thompson
Builder: John Thompson
Photo: ca. 1960, George Gould

Originally this barn had a square cupola, but a tornado destroyed it after this photo was taken. The 46-foot-diameter barn has a poured-concrete foundation and a sectional cone roof covered with metal sheeting. It was built as a hog barn and is still being used for that purpose.

Greene County

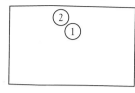

28-1: *TRUE-CIRCULAR BARN*

BUILT: ca. 1907
(destroyed, 1981)
SITE: Jefferson Township
ORIGINAL OWNER: J. A. Gaskill
ARCHITECT/BUILDER: unknown
PHOTO: ca. 1968, Gene Worl

This was one of four concrete-block round barns built in Indiana. Measuring 70 feet across, it could hold 50 cattle and eight horses. It had a conical roof topped with a cupola that was eventually removed. The barn cost $1,000 to build. Its picture and description appeared in a 1907 issue of the *Indiana Farmer*.

28-2: *TRUE-CIRCULAR BARN*

BUILT: 1914
SITE: Jefferson Township
ORIGINAL OWNER: William Easter
BUILDERS: Cliff Drake and Claude Miller
PHOTO: 1985

Of three poured-concrete barns built in Indiana, this is the only one to utilize metal compression rings to hold the walls up. It is a bank barn with a central, poured-concrete silo and a conical roof topped with a small cupola. The barn is no longer in use.

Hamilton County

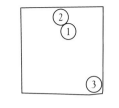

29-1: *TRUE-CIRCULAR BARN*

BUILT: 1906–07
(destroyed by fire, 1991)
SITE: Jackson Township
ORIGINAL OWNER: William Malott
ARCHITECT: probably Horace Duncan or Isaac McNamee
BUILDER: Leander Kellam
PHOTO: 1987, Joe H. Burgess (Courtesy Hamilton County Historical Society)

Malott paid money for the right to build this barn. Since the circular barn was patented by Horace Duncan and Isaac McNamee, Malott probably bought the design from one of them. The barn measured 60 feet in diameter and had a north-south driveway. A rectangular gable-roofed entry was located on the south side, and a silo was located next to the entry. The round cupola was 10 feet high and 15 feet in diameter.

29-2: *TRUE-CIRCULAR BARN*

BUILT: 1906–07
(destroyed by tornado, 1965)
SITE: Jackson Township
ORIGINAL OWNER: George Peppin
ARCHITECTS: probably Horace Duncan and Isaac McNamee
BUILDER: Leander Kellam
PHOTO: ca. 1960s, photographer unknown (Courtesy Marie Gwinn)

Tornadoes have always threatened farm structures in Indiana. This is one of three round barns destroyed by the famous Palm Sunday tornadoes that hit north central Indiana in 1965. It is said that this barn was copied from the Malott circular barn (#29-1) located a mile away.

29-3: *TRUE-CIRCULAR BARN*

BUILT: 1904
(destroyed by tornado, 1948)
SITE: Fall Creek Township
ORIGINAL OWNER: Floyd Whetsal
ARCHITECT/BUILDER: Benton Steele
PHOTO: date and photographer unknown (Courtesy Nelle Hoss)

The original blueprints of this barn still exist, consisting of four plans, a lumber bill, and carpenter's specifications. All were prepared by Benton Steele. The four blueprints showed plans of the elevation, the lower-level floor, the second-level floor, and the roof. The carpenter's specifications gave instructions on how to build the barn. The Whetsal barn was 60 feet in diameter with an east-west driveway. The self-supporting roof had a circular hay track, which was probably supplied by the Louden Machinery Company of Fairfield, Iowa.

Hancock County

30-1: *True-Circular Barn*

Built: 1916
Site: Vernon Township
Original owner: Lulu Swartz
Builder: Frank Woodbury
Photo: 1961, George Gould

This 60-foot-diameter circular barn is one of two built by the Swartz and Dunham families. A silo is located on the west side, and the round cupola was once twice as tall as it is now. The two-pitch gambrel roof is self-supporting. Originally, horses and cattle were sheltered here. The famous Littleton round barn (#30-2) located a couple miles away probably influenced the Swartz-Dunham barns. The current owner has converted the barn into a beautiful house.

30-2: *True-Circular Barn*

Built: ca. 1903
Site: Vernon Township
Original owner:
Frank L. Littleton
Architect: Benton Steele
Builders: Isaac McNamee,
Horace Duncan, and Jim Sears
Photo: 1985

Littleton's magnificent barn is the one that helped initiate the round-barn craze in Indiana and the Midwest. Its construction brought together a number of entrepreneurs who would go on to patent and promote the circular-barn concept. Photographs and descriptions of this barn were widely circulated, and the Littleton barn was featured in Benton Steele's promotions as the Ideal Circular Barn. Horace Duncan and Isaac McNamee went on to use Littleton's legal expertise to patent their "Self-supporting Conical Roof" in 1905. At 102 feet in diameter, this is the largest round barn in Indiana. It has a ramp leading to the hay mow, which can hold 350 to 400 tons of hay. Originally, the barn had a 16-foot-diameter windmill that pumped water and supplied power for machinery; however, it blew off shortly after it was erected and was never rebuilt. Only three circular barns in Indiana are known to have had windmills constructed in this

manner. Littleton's barn design was intended to provide storage room and quarters for all the feed and stock that could be produced on a 240-acre farm while allowing for growth and improvement in years to come. The barn is still in use and is in great shape. For additional information, see Benton Steele, "A Circular Barn," *Indiana Farmer*, Jan. 9, 1902; and Steele's "New Type Of Circular Barn," in *Farm Buildings* (Chicago: *Breeder's Gazette*, 1913).

30-3: *True-Circular Barn*

Built: 1910
(destroyed by windstorm, 1988)
Site: Vernon Township
Original owner:
Frank Dunham
Builders: Hiram and
Frank Dunham
Photo: 1985

In 1910 Frank Dunham was in need of a new barn to accompany his new house. Being a practical man, he saw all of the merits and efficiencies of the Littleton barn (#30-2), located a short distance away. Not as well-off financially as Littleton, Dunham decided to build a smaller barn, a 50-foot-diameter version with a north-south driveway; a self-supporting, two-pitch gambrel roof; and a circular hay track.

30-4: *Octagonal Barn*

Built: ca. 1890
Site: Brown Township
Original owner: John Fort
Architect/Builder: unknown
Photo: 1986

Very little is known about this barn; however, its historical significance could be great. Located between Warrington and Willow Springs in eastern Hancock County, this barn may have contributed to Benton Steele's interest in circular barns. Steele grew up in this area, and he was surely aware of this unusual octagonal barn. Perhaps he even helped build it. The Fort barn and the octagonal house located a half mile north that was owned by Steele's great-aunt, Jane Ross Reeves, probably sowed the seeds that later sparked his interest in the round-barn concept.

30-5: *True-Circular Barn*

Built: 1901
(destroyed by fire, 1940s)
Site: Brown Township
Original owner:
John W. Whisler
Architect: probably
Benton Steele
Builders: Isaac and
Emery McNamee
Photo: date unknown,
from a drawing by C. A.
Hartman (Courtesy John H.
Whisler)

This round barn was the second one that the McNamees built. Its construction introduced Benton Steele to the McNamees. In a 1905 letter, John Whisler wrote to Benton Steele: "I am greatly pleased with my round barn. It is so well arranged and affords much more space than a rectangular barn; besides, it proved more economical to build, considering the increased capacity gained by the circular formation. When the cyclone passed through here . . . the only damage done to my barn was a few shingles ripped off, while nearly every barn in the neighborhood was totally destroyed." The 1902 tornado Whisler referred to brought the builders fame and earned the round barn its cyclone-proof reputation.

Harrison County

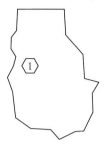

31-1: OCTAGONAL BARN

BUILT: pre-1900
SITE: Tippecanoe Township
ORIGINAL OWNER:
possibly Wurm
ARCHITECT/BUILDER: unknown
PHOTO: 1969, Gene Worl

Originally, this barn had a ramp leading to the hay mow; however, between 1970 and 1980 the upper level caved in, and a sectional cone roof was placed on top of the first level. It's likely that this may have been one of the first octagonal barns built in Indiana. It closely resembles one of those advertised by Elliott Stewart, the octagonal barn promoter from Buffalo, New York.

Henry County

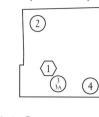

33-1: OCTAGONAL BARN

BUILT: 1874 (razed, 1973)
SITE: Greensboro Township
ORIGINAL OWNER:
Nathan Pearson Henley
ARCHITECT: probably
Elliott Stewart
BUILDER:
Nathan Pearson Henley
PHOTO: 1964, George Gould

The Henley barn was the first circular barn built in Indiana. It was probably copied from the design that Elliott Stewart published in the Buffalo, New York, *Live-Stock Journal* in 1874. This barn was probably the talk of the town when it was constructed. It had a self-supporting, sectional-cone slate roof; a ramp providing access to the second level; vertical wood siding; and a large rectangular annex. Unfortunately, after years of withstanding winter storms, the roof collapsed in 1973, and the barn was demolished.

33-2: TRUE-CIRCULAR BARN

BUILT: date unknown
(razed, 1971)
SITE: Fall Creek Township
ORIGINAL OWNER: Emisweller
ARCHITECT: probably
designed by Benton Steele,
Horace Duncan, or Isaac or
Emery McNamee
BUILDER: Charley Wiley
PHOTO: 1968, Gene Worl

The Emisweller barn was the smallest round barn built in Indiana. Measuring only 24 feet in diameter, it had a conical roof and a six- or eight-sided cupola. The original poured-concrete foundation can still be seen. Its proximity to Knightstown and Warrington suggests roots to Benton Steele, Isaac and Emery McNamee, and Horace Duncan.

33-3, 33-3A:
TRUE-CIRCULAR BARN

BUILT: 1902 (razed, 1940s;
replaced with smaller round
barn, 1940s)
SITE: Franklin Township
ORIGINAL OWNER:
H. W. Painter
ARCHITECTS/BUILDERS:
probably Benton Steele and
Isaac and Emery McNamee
PHOTO 1: From *Indiana Farmer*,
Feb. 24, 1906
PHOTO 2: 1987

This barn achieved some popularity in the article "Silo and Barn Combined," which appeared in a 1906 issue of the *Indiana Farmer*. It is not known who built this barn, but the description of it in that article was in typical Benton Steele fashion. Its proximity to Knightstown suggests a link to Emery and Isaac McNamee. The barn had a conical roof, was 54 1/2 feet in diameter, and had a 28x32-foot rectangular annex. Half of the basement level was divided into box stalls for horses with feedways positioned around the interior silo. The other half was used for cows with feedways positioned around the silo and along the outside wall. As a bank barn, access to the hay mow was easy. A circular track and slings were used to load hay into the barn. Sometime in the 1940s the barn was dismantled; reports are that it was still in good shape. It was replaced with the existing round hog barn a short time later. Measuring 40 feet across, this newer barn, which has one level and a sectional cone roof, was built inside the foundation of the first barn. The original poured-concrete foundation and concrete watering trough can still be seen. Additional information on this barn is in Anna Mercy Painter, *A Homespun Quaker Family Chronicle* (Niagara, N.Y.: Niagara Frontier Press, 1970).

33-4: *True-circular barn*

BUILT: 1903
(destroyed by fire, 1944)
SITE: Dudley Township
ORIGINAL OWNER:
Alva Langston
ARCHITECTS: probably
Isaac and Emery McNamee
BUILDER: Alva Langston
PHOTO: 1903,
photographer unknown
(Courtesy Anna Langston)

Alva Langston and his sons built this bank barn. The idea probably originated with the McNamees because they grew up near where the barn was located. The barn measured 75 to 80 feet across and had a self-supporting, two-pitch roof. A silo was located in the center.

Howard County

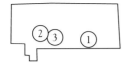

34-1: *True-circular barn*

BUILT: 1909
SITE: Taylor Township
ORIGINAL OWNER:
Lawrence Armfield
BUILDER: Lawrence Armfield
PHOTO: 1986

Armfield's barn measures 60 feet across with a north-south driveway through it. The wood shakes on the original roof were from Oregon; they were replaced from the same origin in the 1950s. The two-pitch gambrel roof has a circular hay track inside. A derrick-like structure inside the barn helps support the roof. Dairy and beef cattle were kept on the east side, and horses were kept on the west side. A track was installed on the east side to move silage from the exterior silo that was once located at the northeast side of the barn.

34-2: *True-circular barn*

BUILT: 1909–13
(destroyed by tornado, 1965)
SITE: Harrison Township
ORIGINAL OWNER:
Benny Hollingsworth
ARCHITECT/BUILDER: unknown
PHOTO: 1954, George Gould

Of the four concrete-block barns built in Indiana, this was the most unusual. It had a main entrance with two decorative pillars, and while most round barns have sliding doors on the outside, the Hollingsworth barn had interior sliding doors with a spring release to help open and close them. The barn was 60 feet across with a self-supporting, two-pitch gambrel roof. Located on State Highway 26, this barn was a landmark for years until the 1965 Palm Sunday tornadoes destroyed it. Remnants of this barn can still be seen today.

34-3: *True-circular barn*

BUILT: 1913
(destroyed by tornado, 1965)
SITE: Harrison Township
ORIGINAL OWNER: Tom Lindley
ARCHITECT/BUILDER: unknown
PHOTO: 1954, George Gould

This barn was a landmark for many years until the Palm Sunday tornadoes destroyed it in 1965. It measured 60 feet across with horizontal wood siding and a 16-foot-diameter central silo. Lindley was a breeder of Percheron horses. A photograph of Lindley's barn appeared in the December 5, 1913, issue of the *Farmer's Guide*.

Huntington County

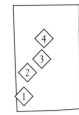

35-1: *Fourteen-sided barn*

BUILT: 1907–08
SITE: Polk Township
ORIGINAL OWNER:
Oliver Perry Watson
BUILDERS: Oliver Perry
Watson and John Smith
PHOTO: 1986

According to the present owner, Oliver Watson's house was built in 1905, and two or three years later the unusual fourteen-sided barn was built. Neighbor John Smith helped, earning 50 cents an hour for his efforts. The main entrance has a gable-roofed hay dormer. The sectional cone roof is topped with an unusual, square, gable-roofed cupola. Inside, sixteen posts are arranged in a circular pattern to help support the roof. One center post also supports the roof. There are three levels inside: the lower level has a feeding trough in the center, and the second and third levels comprise the hay mow. Originally, the barn was used for cattle, then later, for hogs.

35-2: *TWELVE-SIDED BARN*

BUILT: date unknown (dismantled, 1978)
SITE: Polk Township
ORIGINAL OWNER: Yarger or Bouker
ARCHITECT/BUILDER: unknown
PHOTO: 1963, George Gould

This twelve-sided barn measured approximately 50 feet across. It had horizontal wood siding and a sectional, two-pitch gambrel roof topped with a small metal aerator. A gable-roofed overhang sheltered the main entrance. In 1978 the barn was sold for $500, dismantled, and used to build a garage.

35-3: *SIXTEEN-SIDED BARN*

BUILT: 1906
SITE: Huntington Township
ORIGINAL OWNER: S. C. Snyder
BUILDERS: S. C. Snyder and George McFeeley
PHOTO: 1986

The rectangular portion of this barn was built in 1904 by George McFeeley. By 1906, S. C. Snyder, McFeeley's son-in-law, needed additional space, so they added a circular structure. Lumber came from a

sawmill located on the farm. The rectangular section was used to shelter horses, and the round structure was used as a cattle room. Hay and grain were stored in the mow above. The barn has horizontal wood siding, and the self-supporting, three-pitch gambrel roof is topped with a small rectangular cupola. A photograph and description of this barn appeared in the July 11, 1908, issue of the *Farmer's Guide*. The barn was also described in Richard S. Simons, "The Best of Both Barns," *Indianapolis Star Magazine*, Sept. 18, 1977, 23.

35-4: *TWELVE-SIDED BARN*

BUILT: date unknown
SITE: Huntington Township
ORIGINAL OWNER: Fahl
ARCHITECT/BUILDER: unknown
PHOTO: 1986

Located within the city limits of Huntington, this barn was originally built with horizontal wood siding; it has since been covered with new siding. The self-supporting, two-pitch gambrel roof once had a cupola, but it was removed years ago. A north-south driveway passes through the barn, and a rectangular structure was added to the north side a few years ago.

Jackson County

36-1: *TRUE-CIRCULAR BARN*

BUILT: 1910–11
SITE: Driftwood Township
ORIGINAL OWNER: George Stuckwish
BUILDER: Daryl Carter
PHOTO: 1962, George Gould

George Stuckwish patterned his barn after the nearby Mahan barn (#36-2), then in 1913 he decided to buy the Mahan farm. The Schneider sawmill in Ewing, Indiana, furnished all of the beech wood lumber for the Stuckwish barn. Beech wood was thought to help prevent dry rot. The barn cost $1,500; it is 60 feet in diameter with a self-supporting, two-pitch gambrel roof. Mules were sheltered on the south side, and cattle, on the north. An east-west driveway passes through the barn. For more information, see Melissa Stuckwish, "Until One Burned, Stuckwish Farm Had Unique Pair of Barns," *Brownstown Banner*, Feb. 1, 1984; and Betty Baute, "Round Barns of Jackson County," *Watt High Lights,*

Jackson County Rural Electric, vol. 41. no. 5 (Oct. 1986).

36-2: *TRUE-CIRCULAR BARN*

BUILT: 1909–10 (destroyed by fire, 1983)
SITE: Driftwood Township
ORIGINAL OWNER: John Mahan
BUILDER: Louis Geyer
PHOTO: 1962, George Gould

Construction on the Mahan barn began in the fall of 1909 and was completed in 1910. Measuring 70 feet across with an east-west driveway, it was originally equipped with gas lights; electric lights were installed by the 1930s. The round cupola had six windows, and the two-pitch gambrel roof was self-supporting. Mules and cattle were sheltered in the barn. For more information, see the articles by Betty Baute and Melissa Stuckwish.

36-3: *TRUE-CIRCULAR BARN*

BUILT: 1909
SITE: Driftwood Township

ORIGINAL OWNER: John Hess
BUILDER: Louis Geyer
PHOTO: 1985

Construction of the John Hess round barn provided the main impetus for the construction of at least four other circular barns in the area. It is likely that the idea for this barn originated with Benton Steele and his advertisements in the *Indiana Farmer,* but this cannot be confirmed. The Hess barn is 68 feet in diameter with a large central silo similar to those promoted by Benton Steele. The silo helps support the three-pitch gambrel roof. Some years ago the cost of repairing storm damage to the barn was $3,200. The barn is in excellent condition and currently shelters sheep. Additional information on this barn can be found in Betty Baute's article.

36-4: *TRUE-CIRCULAR BARN*

BUILT: ca. 1910
SITE: Carr Township
ORIGINAL OWNER: Howard Smith
BUILDER: Louis Geyer
PHOTO: 1985

"Howard Smith, one of the progressive and prosperous farmers of southern Indiana, . . . has a monstrous big barn with a capacity of over 200 tons of hay and stall capacity for 100 head of cattle. During the big flood of 1913 he stored up to 105 head of livestock from the waters and had room for more. . . . [The barn] is 70 feet high, 72 feet across and 216 feet in circumference. It has a double-hipped roof and is equipped with hay fork, spouts and gutters, lightning rods, a wide, roomy driveway, a veterinary apartment and grain bins. His barn is sprayed with lime-sulfur every few months as a disease eradicator and as a protection against contagious diseases" (excerpts from L. A. Pinchon, "Alfalfa Growing Adds to Livestock Feeder's Profits," *Farmer's Guide*, Sept. 25, 1915). Paul Strom provided an excellent case history and description of this barn in 1980 as part of his graduate studies at Ball State University. Excerpts from this study indicate: ". . . it is believed to have cost a sum of $2,400 for lumber, which was cut green by a local sawmill and erected into place shortly thereafter to take advantage of the natural moisture content of the wood."

36-5: OCTAGONAL BARN

BUILT: ca. 1908 (destroyed, date unknown)
SITE: unknown
ORIGINAL OWNER: unknown
ARCHITECT/BUILDER: unknown
PHOTO: not available

According to a 1908 article in the *Farmer's Guide*, an octagonal barn once stood in Jackson County. Details are not known.

Jay County

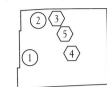

38-1: TRUE-CIRCULAR BARN

BUILT: 1913
SITE: Knox Township
ORIGINAL OWNER: Holdcraft
ARCHITECT/BUILDER: unknown
PHOTO: 1985

This barn is very dark inside because it only has one main entrance, four small windows, and a small metal aerator instead of a cupola. It is a small barn, about 50 feet in diameter, built on a poured-concrete foundation. The two-pitch gambrel roof has flared eaves and asbestos shingles. At one time it housed 40 cattle around a central feeder.

38-2: TRUE-CIRCULAR BARN

BUILT: 1908
SITE: Penn Township

ORIGINAL OWNER: Rebecca Rankin
ARCHITECT: possibly Benton Steele
BUILDER: Cameron Watt
PHOTO: 1986

Cameron Watt was a carpenter who lived north of Fiat, Indiana. He was hired by Rebecca Rankin in 1908 to take charge of this barn's construction. It is 50 feet in diameter and has vertical wood siding, a circular hay track, and a cupola with louvered windows. The two-pitch gambrel roof is self-supporting except for a center hay chute that extends to the cupola. A glazed-tile silo stands west of the barn. This barn closely matches one described by Benton Steele in the December 30, 1905, issue of the *Indiana Farmer*, so it is believed that Steele designed the barn. Also, a carpenter shown in an old photograph taken during the construction closely resembles Steele.

38-3: OCTAGONAL BARN

BUILT: 1890 (roof collapsed, 1987)
SITE: Jackson Township
ORIGINAL OWNER: Pursey or Rupple

BUILDER: Pursey
PHOTO: 1985

Measuring 90 feet in diameter, this barn had an earthen ramp that provided access to the hay mow. There was a round window over the large doors at the end of the ramp, and the eight-sided cupola had unusual arched, divided ventilators. The sectional cone roof had slate shingles and was self-supporting. There was a single hay track under the roof. The ground floor was arranged in a circular pattern around a central post. An interesting octagonal chicken house resembling the barn is also present on the farm, and two large octagonal barns were built in Jay County at about the same time as this barn.

38-4: OCTAGONAL BARN

BUILT: 1890–91
SITE: Wayne Township
ORIGINAL OWNER: Jay County commissioner
ARCHITECT/BUILDER: unknown
PHOTO: 1985

The Jay County octagonal Floral Hall barn was opened to the public on September 29, 1891. It has always been owned by the Jay County commissioner and leased to the Jay County Fair Board. The original roof was double-pitched and topped with a cupola that was later re-

moved. All eight roof sections have a dormer near the base; four additional dormers were placed higher up on the roof. The lengths of the eight walls range from 32 feet 8 inches to 33 feet 9 inches. The diameter of the barn is approximately 110 feet, making it the widest circular barn in Indiana, but Frank Littleton's 102-foot-diameter barn (#30-2) is taller and still holds the title of the largest round barn in the state. Additional information on the Floral Hall barn can be found in Michael E. McGeady's, "A Project for the Historical American Buildings Survey: The Round House, Jay County Fair Grounds, Portland, Indiana."

38-5: OCTAGONAL BARN

BUILT: ca. 1950 (razed, 1970s)
SITE: Bear Creek Township
ORIGINAL OWNER: Rittenhouse
ARCHITECT/BUILDER: unknown
PHOTO: 1971, Gene Worl

Little is known about this barn. It was constructed as a hog barn with 10-foot sides and a sectional cone roof. There was no cupola.

Jefferson County

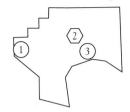

39-1: *TRUE-CIRCULAR BARN*

BUILT: ca. 1911
(razed, 1989–90)
SITE: Graham Township
ORIGINAL OWNER:
possibly Shelton
ARCHITECT/BUILDER: unknown
PHOTO: 1985

Built in an attractive setting with rolling hills, this barn was about 50 feet in diameter with an east-west driveway through the center. It had horizontal wood siding and a self-supporting, two-pitch gambrel roof.

39-2: *OCTAGONAL BARN*

BUILT: early 1880s
(destroyed by tornado, 1974)
SITE: Madison Township
ORIGINAL OWNER: unknown
BUILDER: Moyer
PHOTO: 1970, Gene Worl

This was probably one of the first octagonal barns built in Indiana. It was 80 feet in diameter and 54 feet high with two ramps to the second floor. On the lower level, cattle were kept on the east side, horses on the west side, calves on the south side, and hogs on the north side. It had a sectional cone roof with an octagonal cupola and a small hay dormer. For additional information, see Gordon Englehart, "Barns in the Round," *Louisville Courier-Journal*, Oct. 23, 1966.

39-3: *TRUE-CIRCULAR BARN*

BUILT: ca. 1908
(destroyed by tornado, 1974)
SITE: Madison Township
ORIGINAL OWNER:
George F. Mitchell
ARCHITECT/BUILDER:
probably Horace Duncan
or Emery McNamee
PHOTO: 1970, Gene Worl

This 48-foot-diameter barn had horizontal wood siding, a two-pitch gambrel roof, and a central silo. The barn's distinctive character came from the large hay dormer located above the main entrance. Photographs of this barn appeared in Wilber J. Fraser, *Economy of the Round Dairy Barn*, Bulletin 143 (Urbana, Ill.: University of Illinois Agricultural Experiment Station, Feb. 1910); and in Gordon Englehart, "Barns in the Round," *Louisville Courier-Journal*, Oct. 23, 1966.

Johnson County

41-1: *TRUE-CIRCULAR BARN*

BUILT: 1904
SITE: Union Township
ORIGINAL OWNER: unknown
ARCHITECT/BUILDER:
probably Benton Steele
PHOTO: 1985

In 1951 metal sheeting was used to replace the original vertical wood siding of this circular barn. An east-west driveway passes through the 60-foot-diameter barn. The construction date is inscribed in the foundation. This barn closely resembles Union County barn #81-2, which was built by Benton Steele in 1904.

Knox County

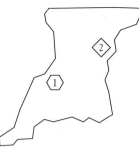

42-1: *OCTAGONAL BARN*

BUILT: 1904 (razed, 1989)
SITE: Palmyra Township
ORIGINAL OWNER:
Henry Decker
BUILDER: Henry Decker
PHOTO: 1986

Henry Decker's octagonal barn was built for cattle feeding. Hayracks were located just inside the walls, and self-feeders were located in the center of the barn. The sectional cone roof had metal sheeting and was topped with a rectangular cupola. The rectangular addition had been constructed on the south side of the barn in the late 1960s or early 1970s.

42-2: *Ten-sided Barn*

Built: ca. 1905
Site: Vigo Township
Original owner: unknown
Architect/Builder: unknown
Photo: 1986

Little is known about this dilapidated barn. It has a sectional cone roof with a small aerator. A photo of this barn appeared in "Stand in the Corner?" *Vincennes Sun-Commercial*, Jan. 19, 1986.

Kosciusko County

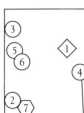

43-1: *Twelve-sided Barn*

Built: 1911
Site: Washington Township
Original owner: Robert Orr
Architects/Builders: Robert Orr and Markemson
Photo: 1987

Helen Oxenrider, the current owner, provided information on this barn: Markemson was a builder who lived next door to Robert Orr. The barn was started in 1911 and completed in 1914. It is a bank barn with vertical wood siding made of sugar maple. The three-pitch gambrel roof is self-supporting. At one time the roof held a circular hay track inside. Entry to the upper level faces south. The barn is currently used for storage.

43-2: *True-circular barn*

Built: 1913
(destroyed by fire, 1975)
Site: Franklin Township
Original owner: Ora Tucker
Architects/Builders: C.V. Kindig and Sons
Photo: ca. 1913, photographer unknown (Courtesy Winifred [Tucker] Smith)

At 82 feet in diameter, this was one of the largest round barns constructed in the Fulton County–Kosciusko County area. It was a bank barn built on a poured-concrete foundation; the lower level was constructed with concrete blocks. The upper level supported a three-pitch gambrel roof. The barn did not have a silo.

43-3: *True-circular barn*

Built: 1910 (razed, 1989)
Site: Scott Township
Original owner: Al Heckeman
Architect/Builder: unknown
Photo: 1985

Until its destruction, this barn was being used as it was when it was built. Work horses and cattle were sheltered on the lower level, and loose hay was stored in the hay mow. The barn measured 60 to 70 feet in diameter; was built on a poured-concrete and concrete-block foundation; and had a self-supporting, two-pitch gambrel roof.

43-4: *True-circular barn*

Built: date unknown
Site: Washington Township
Original owner: unknown
Architect/Builder: unknown
Photo: 1986

The upper level of this 50-foot-diameter bank barn has a west entrance to the hay mow. A circular hay drop is in the center of the mow. The lower level has north and south entrances. Inside the lower level, there is a central hay distribution center. A metal aerator tops the barn, and metal sheeting now covers the barn.

43-5: *True-circular barn*

Built: ca. 1896–1900
(collapsed, 1982)
Site: Etna Township
Original owner: A. A. Gast
Architect/Builder: unknown
Photo: 1980,
Sarah J. De St. Jean

The lower level of this bank barn consisted of flagstone in a concrete matrix. A ramp provided access to the upper level. While most round barns had entrances facing north-south or east-west, the upper entrance of this one faced southwest, and the lower entrance faced northeast.

43-6: *True-circular barn*

Built: ca. 1920
(destroyed by fire, 1965)
Site: Etna Township
Original owner: John Gregg
Architect/Builder: unknown
Photo: not available

This barn was intentionally set on fire because the owner wanted to clear the land for farming. The barn measured about 60 feet across and had vertical wood siding, a driveway through the center, and a round cupola on top.

43-7: OCTAGONAL BARN

BUILT: pre-1900
SITE: Franklin Township
ORIGINAL OWNER: Ora Tucker
ARCHITECT/BUILDER: unknown
PHOTO: 1986

This 35- to 40-foot-diameter hog barn was built by Ora Tucker prior to 1900. After he built his 82-foot circular barn (#43-2) in 1913, he called this eight-sided structure his "little round barn." The octagonal barn is unusual because it is low lying with little or no pitch in its sectional cone roof. The roof is not self-supporting, and there is only one entrance, which is located on the west side of the barn. Information on this barn comes from Winefred (Tucker) Smith of Mentone, Indiana.

LaGrange County

44-1: TWELVE-SIDED BARN

BUILT: 1908
SITE: Newbury Township
ORIGINAL OWNER: Menno S. Yoder
ARCHITECT/BUILDER: Menno S. Yoder
PHOTO: 1970, Gene Worl

This attractive poured-concrete barn was advertised nationally by its designer and owner, Menno S. Yoder. A complete history of its construction was published in several issues of the *Farmer's Guide* between 1908 and 1910. Its construction was also described in *Indiana Farmer, Dakota Farmer, Country Life,* and *Hoard's Dairyman* between 1908 and 1911. Yoder intended to patent this design and sell the plans to interested farmers; however, he was not very successful because his twelve-sided concrete barn is the only one known to exist. Yoder's barn has a two-pitch sectional cone roof, a metal cupola, and a ramp leading to the second level. The total cost of material for this 60-foot-diameter barn was $1,780. It was designed to hold 25 to 30 head of dairy cattle. Today, the barn is a landmark in its area and carries the name "Brown Swiss Dairy."

Lake County

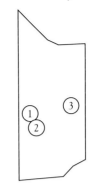

45-1, 45-2:
TWIN TRUE-CIRCULAR BARNS

BUILT: 1909–10
SITE: Hanover Township
ORIGINAL OWNERS: Edward and Julias Echterling
ARCHITECT/BUILDER: Horace Duncan
PHOTO: 1988

This site, consisting of a circular house and two circular barns, is one of the most unusual landmarks in Indiana. Each barn is 40 feet in diameter and has a small hay dormer in the roof. Cupolas originally topped the roofs. One barn, used for cattle, features a 12-foot-diameter silo in the center. The other barn, which does not have a silo, was used primarily for horses, with stalls placed in an unusual rectangular fashion. The house was constructed immediately after the barns. A photograph of the horse barn appeared in the 1910 University of Illinois publication *Economy of the Round Dairy Barn*, and a description of both barns appeared in the May 18, 1912, issue of the *Farmer's Guide*.

45-3: TRUE-CIRCULAR BARN

BUILT: date unknown
SITE: Center Township
ORIGINAL OWNER: F. Meeher or Sam Bold
ARCHITECT/BUILDER: unknown
PHOTO: 1986

A large hay dormer above the main entrance characterizes this barn. Inside, there is a single hay track leading from the dormer to the center of the barn. A 38-foot-circumference silo was once located in the center, but it was removed years ago. A metal aerator is located on top of the two-pitch roof; it replaced a cupola that was removed in the 1960s. The barn is in excellent condition.

LaPorte County

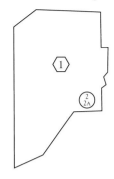

46-1: *Nine-sided barn*

Built: 1878
Site: Pleasant Township
Original owner:
Marion Ridgway
Architect: Marion Ridgway
Builder: Anderson
Photo: 1988

Marion Ridgway was a breeder of Hambletonian and Norman horses and shorthorn cattle. First he built a beautiful home in LaPorte, then in 1878 he constructed the famous nine-sided Door Prairie barn on his farm to the south. It was the second circular barn constructed in Indiana. The barn has a central feeding area, a north entrance, and stall doors in each of the eight remaining sides. A transom above each door was built to add ventilation. A large hay dormer was built above the main entrance

to give maximum access to the loft. The sectional cone roof has an unusually tall cupola with decorative louvers. The 50-foot-diameter barn is constructed on an earthen and fieldstone foundation. In the early days, the names of the horse breeds that Ridgway handled were spelled out in large letters across the front of the barn, an early example of outdoor billboard advertising. While this barn has been publicized in numerous articles and stories, the best account is found in William G. Hope, "Door Prairie Barn" (poster), (LaPorte, Ind.: privately printed, ca. 1980).

46-2, 46-2A:
True-circular barn

Built: 1917–18 (destroyed by fire, 1920; rebuilt, 1921)
Site: Johnson Township
Original owners: James Young, Sr., and James Clark
Architect/Builder: unknown
Photo: 1986

Originally used for work horses and cattle, this barn is now used for storage. It burned down in 1920, but it was rebuilt in 1921. It is 62 feet in diameter with a central, plaster-lined silo that is held together with metal compression rings.

Madison County

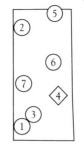

48-1: *True-circular barn*

Built: ca. 1902 (razed, 1975)
Site: Green Township
Original owner:
Otis Grant Battain
Architects: probably Frank Detraz and Benton Steele
Builder: John Rider
Photo: 1961, George Gould

Frank Detraz and Benton Steele probably designed this barn, located only a few miles from their Pendleton headquarters. The entrance matched that shown in Detraz and Steele, "The Circular Ideal Barn," *Indiana Farmer*, Feb. 14, 1903, 1. The barn measured 76 feet across, originally had a cupola and a circular hay track, and could hold 65 head of cattle. It was designed to hold 100 tons of hay, which was baled in the barn, trucked to Pendleton, then shipped by rail to Canada. The silo, located on the southwest side of the barn, still stands.

48-2: *True-circular barn*

Built: date unknown
(razed, ca. 1975–84)
Site: Duck Creek Township
Original owner:
possibly Harry Sells
Architect/Builder: unknown
Photo: 1968, Gene Worl

This 60-foot-diameter barn had a metal roof, a metal aerator, and siding constructed of red tile and brick. This was the only round barn in Indiana constructed with this material. The roof was supported by a center post and six posts arranged in a circular pattern.

48-3: *True-circular barn*

Built: ca. 1902
Site: Stoney Creek Township
Original owner: Jim Sears
Architects/Builders:
Benton Steele, Frank Detraz, Isaac and Emery McNamee, and Jim Sears
Photo: 1969, Gene Worl

Jim Sears helped build the 102-foot-diameter Littleton barn (#30-2) located a few miles to the south of his farm, the Sears Stock Farm. When it was

time for Sears to build, he chose a smaller, 76-foot-diameter version. Inside is a 16-foot-diameter silo. On the east side, a rectangular attachment encloses the original homestead log cabin. Steele is believed to be the architect of the barn because the interior closely resembles one described by him in the November 30, 1907, issue of the *Indiana Farmer*. The barn was also mentioned in "Cyclone Proof: Cyclones Have No Disastrous Effect on Cylindrical Barns," *Anderson Morning Herald*, Feb. 20, 1903, 3.

48-4: *Ten-sided barn*

Built: 1914
Site: Union Township
Original owner:
E. D. Sphenger
Architect/Builder: unknown
Photo: 1986

Located on Valley Grove Farm, this ten-sided barn closely resembles one built in Shelby County (#73-1). The Sphenger barn is 50 feet in diameter and has a sectional cone roof, horizontal wood siding, and a large hay dormer on the south side. Built on a poured-concrete and concrete-block foundation, the barn is still used as originally planned, for horse breeding.

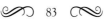

48-5: TRUE-CIRCULAR BARN

BUILT: 1903

SITE: Boone Township

ORIGINAL OWNER: Dr. Horace Jones

ARCHITECTS: Frank Detraz and Benton Steele

BUILDERS: Isaac McNamee and Horace Duncan

PHOTO: 1986

In the February 14, 1903, issue of the *Indiana Farmer*, Detraz and Steele described the "Circular Ideal Barn." Later that year, Dr. Horace Jones of Summitville hired Isaac McNamee and Horace Duncan to build a barn of the same design but with a few extra features. Jones added a 15-foot-wide wing, which encircled half of the 70-foot-diameter barn on the east side. Later, two glazed-tile silos were placed on the north side.

48-6: TRUE-CIRCULAR BARN

BUILT: ca. 1905

SITE: Jackson Township

ORIGINAL OWNER: Noah Whetsal

ARCHITECT/BUILDER: probably Benton Steele

PHOTO: 1971, Gene Worl

Two nearly identical, rectangular gambrel-roofed entrances on the north and south give this barn its character. Measuring 60 feet across, it has a self-supporting, two-pitch gambrel roof and an unusual cupola with lattices instead of windows. Benton Steele probably built this barn because he built one a few miles away in Hamilton County for Floyd Whetsal (#29-3) in 1904.

48-7: TRUE-CIRCULAR BARN

BUILT: ca. 1898 (dismantled, 1989)

SITE: Jackson Township

ORIGINAL OWNER: Henry Kemp

ARCHITECT: probably Franklin H. King

PHOTO: 1986

This was one of the first true-circular barns built in Indiana. Except for only having an entry to the lower level, this barn closely resembled that designed by Professor Franklin H. King of the University of Wisconsin Agricultural Experiment Station. The barn was about 80 feet in diameter and had a conical roof supported by a central silo and 16 posts.

Marion County

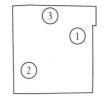

49-1: TRUE-CIRCULAR BARN

BUILT: 1909 (razed, ca. 1979)

SITE: Lawrence Township

ORIGINAL OWNER: John M. Barbour

ARCHITECT/BUILDER: Horace Duncan

PHOTO: 1962, George Gould

Barbour was a state senator and a farmer. As a subscriber to the *Indiana Farmer*, he was familiar with Benton Steele's round-barn promotions. Convinced by the circular idea, he decided to build one on his farm east of Indianapolis. Since Benton Steele had recently moved to Kansas, Horace Duncan was hired to construct the barn. Heavy timber used in the structure was cut from a farm owned by Barbour in Decatur County. The barn measured 60 feet in diameter and stood 60 feet high. A driveway through the barn was 12 feet wide, long enough to park four wagons. The hay mow could hold 100 tons of hay. The barn was originally used as a horse stable and then converted to a dairy barn. Once a prominent landmark on Interstate 465 on the east side of Indianapolis, it was torn down around 1979. The Loft Inn on Shadeland Avenue now stands in its place. For additional information, see Frank Salzarulo, "39 Year Old Round Barn Ideal for Dairy Use," *Indianapolis News*, 1948.

49-2: TRUE-CIRCULAR BARN

BUILT: 1908 (razed, ca. 1960)

SITE: Decatur Township

ORIGINAL OWNER: Wymond J. Beckett

ARCHITECT/BUILDER: probably Benton Steele

PHOTO: 1961, George Gould

This was the second circular barn built by Wymond J. Beckett, the affluent Indianapolis attorney. Steele built the first one, and he probably built this one, too. It was a bank barn with a large rectangular annex. A silo was located in the center. The barn was originally used to raise Angus cattle, but it was later converted to a dairy barn. It was torn down just prior to the construction of Interstate 465 on the south side of Indianapolis.

The barn is described in Fred D. Cavinder, "Barn in the Round," *Indianapolis Star Magazine*, Oct. 22, 1961.

49-3: TRUE-CIRCULAR BARN

BUILT: date unknown (razed, ca. 1960)

SITE: Pike Township

ORIGINAL OWNER: F. D. L.

ARCHITECT/BUILDER: unknown

PHOTO: 1957, George Gould

Little is known about this barn. It appears to have been 50 to 60 feet in diameter with a two-pitch gambrel roof. The Pyramids, an office complex in northern Indianapolis, now stands on the site. The name of the original owner is not known; however, the initials F. D. L. were painted over the main entry. The woodwork suggested links to the McNamees and Steele.

Marshall County

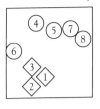

50-1: *Twelve-Sided Barn*

Built: 1913–14
(razed, 1985–86)
Site: Green Township
Original owner:
John Leland, Sr.
Builder: Lawson Leland
Photo: 1969, Gene Worl

Lawson Leland, the brother of this barn's owner, John Leland, was a carpenter. From 1912 to 1914, he and the rest of the Leland family built three nearly identical round barns (#50-1, #50-2, and #50-3). All were twelve-sided bank barns with central silos. Twelve-sided cupolas topped the sectional two-pitch roofs. The barns, each about 56 feet in diameter, were used for dairy purposes and to shelter horses. The Leland barns represented one of the many clusters of round barns built in Indiana. Often these clusters were due to a family such as the Lelands, who would obtain a plan from an agricultural journal or an acquaintance and build it themselves.

50-2: *Twelve-Sided Barn*

Built: 1912
Site: Green Township
Original owner:
possibly Lloyd Leland
Builder: Lawson Leland
Photo: 1985

This attractive barn is in good shape; however, the farm is abandoned and its future is uncertain. This barn gained some publicity in "A Twelve Sided Barn," *Farmer's Guide*, May 30, 1914: "It is 56 feet in diameter, with an 8½ foot basement and 20 feet of siding above the basement. . . . The roof is self-supporting, resting only on the (purlin) plate. . . . The silo is 12 by 41 feet, 11 feet being of cement and is the support for the main floor of the barn. Above the main floor it is a stave silo. . . . Mr. Leland says, 'This barn can be built cheaper than a square or rectangular barn of the same size, as it takes less than two-thirds as much frame, less foundation wall, siding, paint and roofing. The roof is a little more expensive as there is some waste in cutting, also it is more work to build.'"

50-3: *Twelve-Sided Barn*

Built: 1913–14
Site: Green Township
Original owner:
Clarence Quivey
Builder: Lawson Leland
Photo: 1985

The last of three barns built by Lawson Leland, this one is characterized by its numerous rectangular attachments that were added in the 1930s when it was converted to a dairy barn. Thirty-five cattle could be milked at once.

50-4: *True-Circular Barn*

Built: date unknown
Site: North Township
Original owner:
possibly Fay Martin
Builder: probably
Philip Lauderman
Photo: 1985

Little is known about this barn. It resembles barn #50-5 and therefore was probably built by Philip Lauderman. The barn measures 60 feet across and has a north-south driveway and a three-pitch gambrel roof. It is in good shape, but it is no longer used. A large rectangular addition is located on the north side of the barn.

50-5: *True-Circular Barn*

Built: 1911 (relocated, 1991)
Site: German Township
Original owner:
Frank Aker, Sr.
Builder: Philip Lauderman
Photo: 1985

This is one of several northern Indiana circular barns built by Philip Lauderman of Breman, Indiana. He probably obtained the idea and plans from Benton Steele because Lauderman's barns closely resemble those described by Steele in the *Indiana Farmer*. Also, one of Lauderman's barns was constructed only a short distance from a documented Steele barn. During the construction of the Aker barn, Lauderman set up jigs in the barnyard, which were used to cut and fit green timbers. When seasoned, they were put into place by use of scaffolds, boom poles, ropes, pulleys, and horses. The barn measures 60 feet across, and the self-supporting, three-pitch gambrel roof has a 15-foot-diameter cupola. The barn was moved to Amish Acres in Nappanee, Indiana, in 1991 and is now used as a theater.

50-6: *True-Circular Barn*

Built: 1911
Site: West Township
Original owner:
George W. Ramsey
Architect/Builder: unknown
Photo: 1986

When Ramsey built his round dairy barn, it cost more than he anticipated. As a result, he had to sell his farm. The 60-foot-diameter bank barn originally had a silo in the center; however, it was removed years ago. Lumber came from the farm and was cut by a portable saw. The barn now shelters livestock.

50-7: *TRUE-CIRCULAR BARN*

BUILT: date unknown
(razed, date unknown)

SITE: German Township

ORIGINAL OWNER: unknown

ARCHITECT/BUILDER: unknown

PHOTO: not available

According to the Marshall County agricultural extension agent and Frank Aker, Jr., the current owner of barn #50-5, a round barn once stood on a farm that is currently owned by William Town of Bremen, Indiana. Details of the structure are not known.

50-8: *TRUE-CIRCULAR BARN*

BUILT: 1912
(razed, date unknown)

SITE: unknown

ORIGINAL OWNER:
Bryan B. Williams

ARCHITECT/BUILDER:
Bryan B. Williams

PHOTO: From Bryan B. Williams, "A Round Barn," *Farmer's Guide*, Aug. 23, 1913

An article written by the owner in a 1913 issue of the *Farmer's Guide* describes this barn: "[It] is 50 feet in diameter, sets on a 2-foot wall of concrete and cobble stones. It is 22 feet high to the eaves, and has a double hip roof. It has horse and cow stables and the mow is floored with matched flooring except a place 12 by 18 feet where I (Mr. Williams) drive in with hay. It is equipped with a round 30-foot track and the Yoder merry-go-round hay carrier with the Goshen side draft hay outfit, which lays the hay in the mow 16 feet from the outside of the barn. . . . I have a hay chute in the center of the barn and all stock faces the center which makes it handy to hay."

Miami County

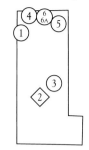

52-1: *TRUE-CIRCULAR BARN*

BUILT: 1914

SITE: Allen Township

ORIGINAL OWNER: John Weller

ARCHITECTS/BUILDERS:
C. V. Kindig and Sons

PHOTO: 1985

This 80-foot-diameter barn is unusual because it was built without a cupola and because the interior silo is not in the center of the barn. Built with native oak beams and soft yellow pine, this bank barn can hold 500 hogs or 100 cattle comfortably. The barn is still in use.

52-2: *TWELVE-SIDED BARN*

BUILT: 1912 (razed, 1981)

SITE: Washington Township

ORIGINAL OWNERS:
Roscoe and Mark Borden

BUILDER: Mark Borden

PHOTO: 1960, George Gould

The two silos that were once located next to this unusual barn have the date of construction inscribed on the concrete foundation. The numerous rectangular additions gave this barn a busy look. It had an east-west driveway through the center and a sectional, three-pitch gambrel roof.

52-3: *TRUE-CIRCULAR BARN*

BUILT: date unknown
(razed, 1970s)

SITE: Erie Township

ORIGINAL OWNER: Gallaham

ARCHITECT/BUILDER: unknown

PHOTO: 1960, George Gould

This is one of four concrete-block round barns constructed in Indiana. In the 1970s, the owner tore it down because the county assessor continued to regard it as a taxable asset even though its walls were cracking and its roof leaked. The barn had a two-pitch gambrel roof and a cupola with louvered windows.

52-4: *TRUE-CIRCULAR BARN*

BUILT: 1912
(destroyed by fire, 1982)

SITE: Allen Township

ORIGINAL OWNER:
Ike B. Mulligan

ARCHITECTS/BUILDERS:
probably C. V. Kindig and Sons

PHOTO: ca. 1970s,
Nettie R. Fisher

Little is known about this barn except that it was similar in design to several other barns in the vicinity of Fulton, Miami, and Kosciusko counties. It is likely that the Kindig builders constructed this one because they built several close by.

52-5: *TRUE-CIRCULAR BARN*

BUILT: ca. 1915

SITE: Perry Township

ORIGINAL OWNER: William Huddleston

ARCHITECTS/BUILDERS: C. V. Kindig and Sons, and Reed Powell

PHOTO: date unknown, from State Aerial Farm Statistics, Mapping Division, Toledo, Ohio (Courtesy Wayne Coplen)

Huddleston sold five acres across the road from where this barn was built in order to finance it. This 60-foot-diameter barn originally had a round cupola, but it was removed in 1976. A circular hay track is located inside, and aluminum siding now covers the vertical wood siding. The foundation is made from poured concrete and concrete blocks layered three high.

52-6, 52-6A: *TRUE-CIRCULAR BARN*

BUILT: 1914 (destroyed by fire, 1915; rebuilt, 1915; razed, 1965)

SITE: Allen Township

ORIGINAL OWNER: Solimon "Gus" Zortman

ARCHITECTS/BUILDERS: C. V. Kindig and Sons, and Reed Powell

PHOTO: date and photographer unknown (Courtesy Lee Southerton)

Before it was ever used, the first barn burned down. Within a year, a new one was erected in its place. This barn was almost exactly like the Huddleston barn (#52-5) except this one had a 10-foot-diameter silo in the center. The Kindigs of Rochester probably built all three barns.

Montgomery County

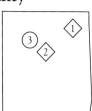

54-1: *TEN-SIDED BARN*

BUILT: 1914

SITE: Sugar Creek Township

ORIGINAL OWNER: William Fisher

BUILDER: Ellsworth Dain

PHOTO: 1986

This unusual 54x56-foot barn has a four- or six-sided cupola. The roof, made of heavy metal sheeting, is the original and is the only one of its kind in Indiana. A north-south driveway passes through the barn. The front and back sides of the barn measure 28 feet across, and each of the remaining eight sides measure 16 feet. Native oak and pine were used to construct the barn.

54-2: *FOURTEEN-SIDED BARN*

BUILT: 1912–13

SITE: Union Township

ORIGINAL OWNER: Wilbur Breeks

BUILDER: George Stout

PHOTO: 1986

Except for four dormers, this barn closely resembles the Chicago Wrecking House Company "Round Barn Design No. 206," which was advertised in the *Indiana Farmer* and other agricultural newspapers between 1910 and 1915. The barn has a north-south driveway and a rare sunken stall, which may have been used to keep a bull. The original horizontal wood siding was made of pine; aluminum siding now covers the barn.

54-3: *TRUE-CIRCULAR BARN*

BUILT: ca. 1910 (razed, ca. 1974)

SITE: Coal Creek Township

ORIGINAL OWNER: Dick "Boss" Thomas

ARCHITECT/BUILDER: unknown

PHOTO: 1962, George Gould

This barn was 60 feet in diameter with a central silo. When built, a time capsule was placed inside; when the barn was torn down, the capsule was retrieved, but its contents were kept secret.

Morgan County

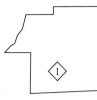

55-1: *SIX-SIDED BARN*

BUILT: date unknown
SITE: Washington Township
ORIGINAL OWNER: unknown
ARCHITECT/BUILDER: unknown
PHOTO: 1985

One of three circular barns in Indiana with six sides, this barn has a north-south entrance and a sectional cone roof. There is no silo or cupola.

Newton County

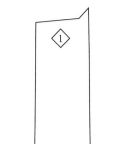

56-1: *EIGHTEEN-SIDED BARN*

BUILT: 1906
(destroyed, date unknown)
SITE: Lake Township
ORIGINAL OWNER: C. B. Davis
BUILDER: C. B. Davis
PHOTO: From C. B. Davis, "A Good Round Barn," *Indiana Farmer*, Apr. 14, 1906

In a 1906 issue of *Indiana Farmer*, C. B. Davis described and presented plans for his eigh-teen-sided, four-level hog barn. The first level had 15 pens, each with a door leading to the outside. In the middle, there were eight farrowing pens, which were kept warm in the winter by a stove located in the center of the barn. The second floor had four feed bins and a circular hay track. The third floor was used for machine storage, and the fourth floor was used for general storage. Elevators provided easy access to each floor.

Noble County

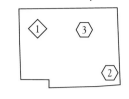

57-1: *SIXTEEN-SIDED BARN*

BUILT: 1911
SITE: Perry Township
ORIGINAL OWNERS:
Ellis and Ralph Smith
ARCHITECTS/BUILDERS:
probably C. V. Kindig and Sons
PHOTO: 1985

Ralph Smith got the idea to build a circular barn while attending agricultural classes at Purdue University. He hired an experienced round-barn builder from Rochester, Indiana, who is believed to be one of the Kindig builders. Each side of the barn is 12 feet long, and the 14-foot-diameter central silo is made of tongue-and-groove cypress. A six-foot feed alley surrounds the silo. The five entries have doors that slide up and down, and the 16-sided cupola has four glass panes and eight louvers. This unusual barn is in excellent shape.

57-2: *OCTAGONAL BARN*

BUILT: date unknown
(destroyed by fire, 1969)
SITE: Swan Township
ORIGINAL OWNER:
Charles Sloane
ARCHITECT/BUILDER: unknown
PHOTO: 1964, George Gould

This bank barn was approximately 60 feet in diameter with a small metal cupola and wood siding. Access to the upper level faced east. The barn was probably constructed prior to 1900.

57-3: OCTAGONAL BARN

BUILT: 1976
SITE: Orange Township
ORIGINAL OWNERS:
Dan and Gene Replogle
ARCHITECTS/BUILDERS:
Dan and Gene Replogle
PHOTO: 1991, Dan Replogle

This barn was constructed after the owner's rectangular barn burned down. Support posts from the rectangular barn were used to build the new octagonal barn. In the tradition of true-circular barns, it has a central feeding area and a hay mow for storage. The barn measures 35 feet across.

Orange County

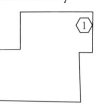

59-1: TRUE-CIRCULAR BARN

BUILT: 1907 (razed, 1974)
SITE: French Township
ORIGINAL OWNER:
George Charles
ARCHITECT/BUILDER:
Benton Steele
PHOTO: 1970, Gene Worl

While standing, this was one of the most picturesque round barns in Indiana. Built by Benton Steele, this 80-foot-diameter bank barn had a three-pitch gambrel roof supported by a central silo. A picture of this barn taken while under construction appeared in the March 13, 1909, issue of the *Indiana Farmer*. Additional information on this barn can be found in Gordon Englehart, "Barns in the Round," *Louisville Courier-Journal*, Oct. 23, 1966.

Owen County

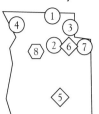

60-1: OCTAGONAL BARN

BUILT: 1912
SITE: Harrison Township
ORIGINAL OWNER:
Gaylord Asher
ARCHITECT/BUILDER:
Fleetwood Truax
PHOTO: 1985

At 36 feet in diameter, this circular barn is one of the smallest in Indiana. Its central silo extends through the roof. There are five windows, one of which provides easy access to the hay mow. The barn has horizontal wood siding. Truax is said to have gotten the barn's pattern from Holland. A photo and story about this barn appeared in "Round Barn in Owen County," *Owen Leader*, Feb. 20, 1986.

Parke County

61-1: TRUE-CIRCULAR BARN

BUILT: 1910 (razed, 1980)
SITE: Sugar Creek Township
ORIGINAL OWNER:
Cunningham
BUILDER: Cunningham
PHOTO: 1960, George Gould

Parke County is generally known for its covered bridges; however, at one time there were at least eight round barns in the county. All but two have been destroyed. Built with horizontal wood siding and a central silo, this one had a large unusual front entrance. The three-pitch gambrel roof once had a cupola, but it was removed in 1964.

61-2: TRUE-CIRCULAR BARN

BUILT: 1906 (razed, ca. 1970)
SITE: Washington Township
ORIGINAL OWNER:
Jess McMullin
ARCHITECT/BUILDER:
Ora Newlin
PHOTO: 1965, George Gould

When Newlin built this barn, he was paid a dollar per day plus room and board. He would leave the site during the week and return on weekends. This 60-foot-diameter barn had horizontal wood siding, a poured-concrete foundation, and a 10-foot-diameter cupola. It originally sheltered horses, but it was later converted to a dairy barn. The original roof cost about $90 to shingle. In the late 1960s, the lowest quote on fixing the roof was $3,000.

61-3: *TRUE-CIRCULAR BARN*

BUILT: ca. 1904
(destroyed by fire, 1986)
SITE: Howard Township
ORIGINAL OWNER: Demaree
ARCHITECT:
possibly Benton Steele
BUILDER: possibly Ora Newlin
PHOTO: 1986

This beautiful barn accidently burned down in April 1986. It was 80 feet in diameter with an east-west central driveway and a self-supporting roof. In the late 1940s, a tornado destroyed the original roof; the photograph shows the replacement. This barn closely resembles some built by Benton Steele, and it is possible he designed this one.

61-4: *TRUE-CIRCULAR BARN*

BUILT: 1895
SITE: Liberty Township
ORIGINAL OWNER:
Robert F. Thompson

ARCHITECT: Franklin H. King
PHOTO: 1986

This barn is believed to be the first true-circular barn constructed in Indiana. It closely resembles the round barn designed in 1889 by Franklin H. King of the University of Wisconsin Agricultural Experiment Station. Like King's design, this barn has horizontal wood siding, a tall cupola, and a conical roof. The lower level of this bank barn is constructed with brick. It is one of two round barns left in Parke County.

61-5: *TWELVE-SIDED BARN*

BUILT: 1910
(razed, ca. 1975–85)
SITE: Raccoon Township
ORIGINAL OWNER:
Charles Wolfe
ARCHITECT/BUILDER: unknown
PHOTO: 1970, Gene Worl

This 50-foot-diameter bank barn had a large hay dormer over the main entrance and three smaller dormers on the asphalt-covered roof. The lower level of the barn was constructed of poured concrete, and the upper level had horizontal wood siding. Inside was a small silo and a manure carrier. Cattle were fed grain from an elevator bin on the first floor and hay

from the loft. The entry to the upper level faced south. Timber used in the barn was from an old coal mine tipple located north of the farm.

61-6: *TWELVE-SIDED BARN*

BUILT: 1923
(destroyed by fire, 1963)
SITE: Greene Township
ORIGINAL OWNER:
Albert Collins
BUILDER: Charlie Hall
PHOTO: 1960, George Gould

This attractive bank barn had three stories: a lower level to shelter cattle, a second level for storage, and a third-level hay mow. Inside, corn cribs and a granary surrounded a freestanding silo. The barn was 60 feet in diameter with a self-supporting roof.

61-7: *TRUE-CIRCULAR BARN*

BUILT: date unknown
(destroyed by fire, 1945)
SITE: Greene Township
ORIGINAL OWNER: O. C. Rider
ARCHITECT/BUILDER: unknown
PHOTO: not available

Little is known about this barn. It had horizontal wood sid-

ing, a lower-level entry, and a self-supporting roof. The barn did not have a silo.

61-8: *OCTAGONAL BARN*

BUILT: date unknown
SITE: Penn Township
ORIGINAL OWNER: unknown
ARCHITECT/BUILDER:
probably William Hill
PHOTO: 1988

This small circular barn, located in the town of Bloomingdale, has horizontal wood siding, one lower-level entry, and a self-supporting roof. It does not have a silo. The barn may have been built by William Hill, builder of the first round barn in the Carthage, Indiana, area (#70-8). Hill, a University of Chicago professor, introduced the round-barn concept to Isaac and Emery McNamee in 1900. The McNamees went on to promote the round barn and help bring it to its pinnacle of construction in 1910. Since Hill was the leader of the Bloomingdale Academy after 1905, he may have influenced the construction of this small octagonal barn. The current owner of the property where the barn is located is a niece of William Hill.

Pike County

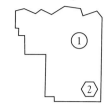

63-1: *TRUE-CIRCULAR BARN*

BUILT: date unknown
(razed, 1945–46)
SITE: Jefferson Township
ORIGINAL OWNER: Hyde Pipes
ARCHITECT/BUILDER: unknown
PHOTO: not available

Reportedly, this barn measured 75 feet across and had north-south entries. The house that was associated with the barn was built in 1874, but it was later torn down. A one-story brick ranch house now sits in its place. No other information is available.

63-2: *OCTAGONAL OR NINE-SIDED BARN*

BUILT: 1914
(collapsed, ca. 1964)

SITE: Lockhart Township

ORIGINAL OWNER:
William Hagemeyer

BUILDER: Otto Brust

PHOTO: date and photographer unknown (Courtesy Mr. and Mrs. Paul Hagemeyer)

Brust used seventeen 100-pound kegs of nails to build this 75-foot-diameter barn. Creek gravel was mixed with cement for the foundation, and when the foundation proved to be defective, it was replaced after the barn was built. The barn had a self-supporting sectional cone roof. According to the current owner, there was a circular hay track that never worked very well. Sixty loads of hay could be stored in the hay mow.

Porter County

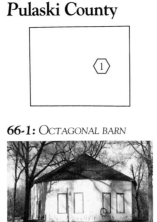

64-1: *TRUE-CIRCULAR BARN*

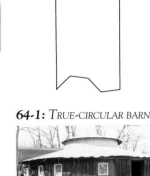

BUILT: 1968

SITE: Westchester Township

ORIGINAL OWNER: unknown

ARCHITECT/BUILDER: unknown

PHOTO: date unknown,
Sarah J. De St. Jean

This is one of the very few modern round barns that have been built. It is currently being used as a horse barn.

Pulaski County

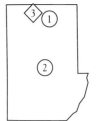

66-1: *OCTAGONAL BARN*

BUILT: ca. 1890
(relocated, 1990)

SITE: Monroe Township

ORIGINAL OWNER:
Pulaski County

ARCHITECT/BUILDER: unknown

PHOTO: 1991

Located on the fairgrounds in Pulaski County, this barn was, at one time, used as a pavilion within the city limits of Winamac. It has vertical wood siding and a sectional cone, self-supporting roof. In 1991, the barn was moved to a more secure foundation about 100 yards from its original site.

Putnam County

67-1: *TRUE-CIRCULAR BARN*

BUILT: date unknown
(destroyed, 1989)

SITE: Franklin Township

ORIGINAL OWNER:
Hart or Smythe

ARCHITECT/BUILDER: unknown

PHOTO: 1986

This barn had horizontal wood siding and an east-west driveway through the middle. A feed track was located on the west side and connected to the silo on the south side. The self-supporting roof may have had a cupola at one time.

67-2: *TRUE-CIRCULAR BARN*

BUILT: 1910–11
(collapsed, 1989)

SITE: Greencastle Township

ORIGINAL OWNER:
Edwin E. Black

ARCHITECT/BUILDER: unknown

PHOTO: 1985

Built on a concrete-block foundation, this barn was 60 feet in diameter, 65 feet high, and had horizontal wood siding. The self-supporting, three-pitch gambrel roof once featured a cupola. A photograph of the barn appeared in the January 23, 1915, issue of the *Farmer's Guide*.

67-3: *SIX-SIDED BARN*

BUILT: date unknown
(razed, date unknown)

SITE: Franklin Township

ORIGINAL OWNER: unknown

ARCHITECT/BUILDER: unknown

PHOTO: 1962, George Gould

This is one of three 6-sided barns known to have been built in Indiana. Little is known about this one except that it was about a mile east of Raccoon on the road to the Cornstalk Covered Bridge in Putnam County.

Randolph County

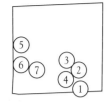

68-1: TRUE-CIRCULAR BARN

BUILT: pre-1905
(roof collapsed, 1990)
SITE: Washington Township
ORIGINAL OWNER:
possibly Starbuck
BUILDER: Sam Bore
PHOTO: 1985

Sawmill owner Sam Bore provided the lumber and building expertise for this 60-foot-diameter bank barn. Its conical roof was self-supporting with a large cupola that measured about 20 feet across. A large rectangular addition was located on the west side.

68-2: TRUE-CIRCULAR BARN

BUILT: 1906
SITE: Washington Township

ORIGINAL OWNER:
Frederick Retter
BUILDERS: Nelson McCollum and Bob Blancett
PHOTO: 1985

Nelson McCollum, a local carpenter, built at least four round barns in the Randolph County area. This was the second one he built for Frederick Retter. Learning from experience, he built this one with a cupola designed to increase air circulation in the barn. A circular hay track was not installed in this barn because Retter found the track in the first one difficult to use. Instead a set of pulleys were installed to help distribute hay in the mow. This barn is 63 feet in diameter, constructed with oak, beech, and other hardwoods. It has a ramp to a large rectangular entrance on the second floor.

68-3: TRUE-CIRCULAR BARN

BUILT: 1905 (razed, 1970s)
SITE: Washington Township
ORIGINAL OWNER:
Frederick Retter
BUILDER: Nelson McCollum
PHOTO: 1961, George Gould

When McCollum built this barn for Retter in 1905, he did not install a cupola. During the winter of 1905–06, Retter stored straw in the hay mow, but it spoiled because the barn had poor air circulation. To rectify this, Retter added four dormers to the roof. Retter made sure his next barn included a cupola. Retter's first barn, shown here, was 63 feet in diameter. It had a circular hay track and a ramp to the rectangular entrance on the second floor of the barn.

68-4: TRUE-CIRCULAR BARN

BUILT: 1908
SITE: Washington Township
ORIGINAL OWNER:
Howard Hormel
BUILDER: probably Nelson McCollum
PHOTO: 1985

Originally this barn's roof was wood shingle, but it was replaced with metal sheeting in 1927. Similarly, the barn originally had horizontal wood siding, but it was replaced with metal siding in 1973. The barn measures 60 feet in diameter and was probably built by Nelson McCollum. It is still used to shelter cattle. For more information, see Max Knight, "Randolph County Has Five Round Barns," *Richmond Palladium-Item*, Nov. 28, 1972.

68-5: TRUE-CIRCULAR BARN

BUILT: pre-1910
SITE: Stoney Creek Township
ORIGINAL OWNER:
George Thompson
ARCHITECT/BUILDER: unknown
PHOTO: 1985

Recently renovated, this barn is one of four in Indiana with this peculiar shape. It is 37 1/2 feet in diameter with a 10-foot-diameter wood-stave silo in the center. The silo has metal compression rings and extends about 10 feet above the roofline. A gable-roofed chute is attached to the silo. The roof is not attached to or supported by the silo, although it appears to be. For more information, see Robert C. Schulz's "Round Barn: Rural Route 1, Parker, Box 351, Windsor Road, Stoney Creek Township, Randolph County, Exterior Description."

68-6: TRUE-CIRCULAR BARN

BUILT: ca. 1905
(destroyed by fire, 1969)
SITE: Union Township

ORIGINAL OWNER:
H. E. Clevenger
ARCHITECT:
probably Benton Steele
BUILDER: Nelson McCollum
PHOTO: From "Round Barn on Farm of H. E. Clevenger, Randolph County," *Indiana Farmer*, Oct. 6, 1906

A photograph of this barn appeared in a 1906 issue of the *Indiana Farmer*. The barn was about 50 feet in diameter with a central silo, a two-pitch gambrel roof, and vertical wood siding. Its main entrance faced east. Nelson McCollum built the barn, and Benton Steele may have designed it.

68-7: TRUE-CIRCULAR BARN

BUILT: date unknown
(razed, 1960s)
SITE: Union Township
ORIGINAL OWNER:
Wright or Hunt
ARCHITECT/BUILDER: unknown
PHOTO: 1961, George Gould

This unusual low-lying barn had a rectangular cupola, a conical roof, and a small 12- to 14-foot-diameter central silo. The barn itself was only 40 feet in diameter.

Ripley County

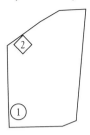

69-1: *True-circular barn*

Built: pre-1915
Site: Shelby Township
Original owner:
Charles Kiefer
Architect/Builder: unknown
Photo: From *Farmer's Guide*,
January 23, 1915

This 50- to 60-foot-diameter barn has vertical wood siding, a north-south driveway, and a conical roof. The cupola no longer exists.

69-2: *Twelve-sided barn*

Built: 1915
Site: Jackson Township
Original owner: Gus Siebert
Architect/Builder: unknown
Photo: 1985

Measuring 50 feet across and 50 feet high, this barn has a sectional, two-pitch gambrel roof and a 12-foot-wide east-west driveway through the barn. A metal aerator tops the roof.

Rush County

70-1: *True-circular barn*

Built: 1927
Site: Washington Township
Original owner:
Frank O. Austill
Architect/Builder:
Emery McNamee
Photo: 1986

Frank Austill was a brother-in-law to round-barn builder Emery McNamee. This barn was probably the last one McNamee built from scratch. It is 50 feet in diameter with a very unusual low-lying cupola. Originally used for cattle and horses, the barn is now used to shelter hogs.

70-2: *True-circular barn*

Built: date unknown
Site: Rushville Township
Original owner: Cullen
Architect/Builder: unknown
Photo: 1985

A cupola once adorned the top of this two-pitch gambrel roof, but it was removed many years ago. This two-story barn has a ramp leading to the second level, and the entry to that level faces west. Little else is known about the barn.

70-3: *True-circular barn*

Built: 1912–13
(destroyed by windstorm, 1980)
Site: Orange Township
Original owner: Will Roth
Builder: Will Roth
Photo: 1973, George Gould

Will Roth was a wealthy farmer and sawmill owner. He reportedly drew up blueprints and began construction on his barn in 1912, but a 1913 flood washed away the timber that was to be used. After the flood, more timber was cut and construction resumed. All boards were soaked in the nearby river, then bent into place. The barn, 70 feet in diameter, was characterized by its numerous windows and steeply pitching roof. There was a freestanding silo inside. The ground floor was used for mules, horses, and shorthorn cattle. Feed was poured through chutes to livestock from the second floor, while hay and fodder were stored on the third floor. This barn received some publicity in Maxine Cox, "Round Barn Restoration Includes 'Spot' for Crafts," and in Henry S. Wood, "Cadillac of Barns: Round Barn Found in Southwestern Indiana," from newspaper clippings of unknown sources and dates.

70-4: *True-circular barn*

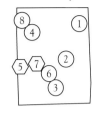

Built: 1911
Site: Posey Township
Original owner: George Price
Architect:
probably F. L. Marsh
Builder: Frank Russ Tweedy
Photo: 1985

F. L. Marsh, a regional expert on farm buildings, probably designed this barn. A

February 10, 1912, article in the *Farmer's Guide* describes a barn that closely resembled this one: "The barn is 48 feet in diameter, and 20 feet high from the foundation to eaves. The lower floor is 7 feet 6 inches high in the clear, and is lined all around to make it doubly warm." Around the drive, horse stalls encompass about three-quarters of the barn. Except for a 300-bushel corn crib, cow stalls make up the remaining one-quarter of space. The sectional cone roof is self-supporting.

70-5: OCTAGONAL BARN

BUILT: 1897
SITE: Walker Township
ORIGINAL OWNERS: Rush County and Paul F. Folger
BUILDERS: Community of Rush County
PHOTO: 1987

Sources indicate that this barn was erected as a horticultural building for the 1897 Rush County Fair. Fruits were displayed in the barn. It was later moved to its present location and converted to a horse barn. There never was a cupola.

70-6: TRUE-CIRCULAR BARN

BUILT: 1906
SITE: Rushville Township
ORIGINAL OWNER: George O. Anderson
BUILDER: Horace Duncan
PHOTO: 1985

This barn, which features an unusual hay dormer on its south side, received publicity in "Practical Barn Plans" written by Anderson in the April 8, 1911, issue of the *Farmer's Guide*.

70-7: OCTAGONAL BARN

BUILT: pre-1916
SITE: Posey Township
ORIGINAL OWNER: James Arnold
ARCHITECT/BUILDER: unknown
PHOTO: 1987

This is one of three circular barns in Indiana built with a windmill extending through the roof. Like the others, the windmill is no longer present; however, a pump was placed inside this barn at a later date to draw water from the well. Used as a hog barn, it requires the support of eight posts to hold up the roof. Its sides are 16 feet long. A rectangular addition is located on the south side. Attractive round vents adorn the cupola.

70-8: TRUE-CIRCULAR BARN
BUILT: 1900 (destroyed, 1930s)
SITE: Ripley Township
ORIGINAL OWNER: William Hill
BUILDERS: Isaac and Emery McNamee
PHOTO: not available

William Hill, a University of Chicago professor and breeder of shorthorn cattle, was very progressive in his ideas. In 1900, he hired Isaac and Emery McNamee to build a round barn with a central silo on his farm in northwestern Rush County. This was the first silo and the first round barn constructed in the area. Hill's barn was important because it launched Isaac and Emery McNamee into the business of building round barns. Hill's barn was believed to be similar to that designed by Professor Franklin H. King of the University of Wisconsin Agricultural Experiment Station. It was approximately 60 feet in diameter with a 20-foot-diameter central silo. Its conical roof probably required support from the silo. A low-lying cupola probably sat on top of the roof. This barn received some publicity in "Cyclone Proof: Cyclones Have No Disastrous Effect on Cylindrical Barns," *Anderson Morning Herald*, Feb. 20, 1903.

St. Joseph County

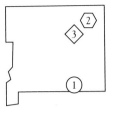

71-1: TRUE-CIRCULAR BARN

BUILT: 1910
SITE: Union Township
ORIGINAL OWNER: John Rouch
BUILDER: probably Philip Lauderman
PHOTO: 1969, Gene Worl

This barn is 56 feet in diameter and 48 feet high with an east-west driveway through its center. The two-pitch gambrel roof is self-supporting. At one time it housed 10 horses, 20 cows, and 20 young cattle. It closely resembles one built by Philip Lauderman in nearby Marshall County, therefore he probably built this one.

71-2: OCTAGONAL BARN

BUILT: 1900
SITE: Harris Township
ORIGINAL OWNERS: Brothers of St. Joseph
ARCHITECTS/BUILDERS: The Reverend Dominic O'Mally and Brother Michael Bergin
PHOTO: 1986

This barn was built for showing cattle, but in the 1940s it was used as a breeding barn for bulls. Today it is used for feeding steers. Inside there was a 20-foot-diameter octagonal silo that was cut off in the lower level when the barn was converted to a breeding pen. It has horizontal wood siding and a low-pitching sectional cone roof.

71-3: SIXTEEN-SIDED BARN

BUILT: ca. 1890 (razed, 1960s)
SITE: German Township
ORIGINAL OWNER: Notre Dame University

ARCHITECT/BUILDER: unknown

PHOTO: date and photographer unknown (Courtesy Brother Carl Tiedt and the Brothers of St. Joseph)

This unusual barn was one of four in Indiana constructed with the silo extending through the roof in this manner. Brother Carl Tiedt says the barn was located on the southwestern corner of the present South Quad on the campus of Notre Dame University, presently the area occupied by Fisher and Pangborn Halls, and the current ninth, tenth, and eleventh holes of the W. J. Burke Memorial Golf Course. He notes that the farm complex included several houses for Brothers and hired hands, the university horse barn, a livery, a dairy barn with a large Holstein herd, a round barn and surrounding sites for raising 700 Hampshire hogs, a hennery, and several grain storage buildings.

Scott County

72-1: OCTAGONAL BARN

BUILT: ca. 1920 (razed, 1982)
SITE: Lexington Township
ORIGINAL OWNER: Bruce F. Hardy
BUILDERS: Bruce F. Hardy family and L. Blocher
PHOTO: 1969, Gene Worl

Bruce, Oliver, and Malta Hardy built four round barns within a few miles of each other between 1916 and 1921. This octagonal barn, about 60 feet in diameter, was used as a hog barn. It had one grand entry and an octagonal cupola. The roof was not self-supporting. A story about this barn appeared in Tim Evans, "Round Barns Still Lure Oddity Seekers," *Columbus* (Ind.) *Republic*, May 18, 1982.

72-2: TRUE-CIRCULAR BARN

BUILT: ca. 1920 (razed, 1990)
SITE: Lexington Township
ORIGINAL OWNER: Oliver Hardy
BUILDERS: Bruce F. Hardy family
PHOTO: 1985

This 36-foot-diameter barn was built around a silo that measured 12 feet in diameter and 36 feet high. It was one of four barns constructed in this manner. On the west side, a gable-roofed dormer topped the silo. Dairy cattle were fed around the silo, then led through a corridor to a large rectangular dairy barn. See Tim Evans's article for more information.

72-3: TRUE-CIRCULAR BARN

BUILT: 1916 (razed, 1982–85)
SITE: Lexington Township
ORIGINAL OWNER: Malta Hardy

BUILDERS: Bruce F. Hardy family
PHOTO: 1969, Gene Worl

This was the first of four round barns built by the Hardy family. Supposedly the plans for this barn came from Purdue University, but this cannot be confirmed. Built as a bank barn and used for dairy purposes, this barn was 70 feet in diameter with a silo in the center. A rectangular milking parlor was located on the east side. See Tim Evans's article for more information.

72-4: OCTAGONAL BARN
BUILT: post-1916 (razed, date unknown)
SITE: Vienna Township
ORIGINAL OWNER: Malta Hardy
BUILDERS: Bruce F. Hardy family
PHOTO: not available

Little is known about this barn except it is said to have been built for hogs and be similar in design to the Bruce F. Hardy barn (#72-1).

Shelby County

73-1: TWELVE-SIDED BARN

BUILT: 1910
SITE: Noble Township
ORIGINAL OWNER: George Rudicel
BUILDERS: George Rudicel and Roy and Earl Henderson
PHOTO: 1985

Similar in design to Madison County barn #48-4, this barn has a gable-roofed dormer over the south entrance and a north-south driveway through the middle. A silo once stood next to the barn, but it was blown away years ago during a windstorm. Lumber for the barn was cut locally and hauled to a nearby sawmill owned by George Howe.

Steuben County

76-1: *TRUE-CIRCULAR BARN*

BUILT: 1917
SITE: Jackson Township
ORIGINAL OWNER:
Channing Barrett
BUILDER: Channing Barrett
PHOTO: 1985

Originally this barn had a cupola, but it was blown off during a 1935 windstorm. In 1945, the roof's cedar shingles were replaced with asphalt shingles. Barn construction is with oak framing and yellow pine siding. The barn is 60 feet in diameter with an 11-foot-diameter silo in the center. It has horizontal wood siding and 23 windows. A ramp provides access to the second floor.

76-2: *TRUE-CIRCULAR BARN*

BUILT: ca. 1916
SITE: Steuben Township
ORIGINAL OWNER:
Cornish Griffin
BUILDERS:
Cornish Griffin family
PHOTO: 1985

This is the only barn in Indiana built with glazed-clay tile. There is also a tiled silo in the center of the 60-foot-diameter barn. Main entrances are located on the northeast and east sides. The two-pitch gambrel roof is self-supporting except for the silo. The glazed-tile cupola, which is actually the upper portion of the silo, has a small dormer on top.

76-3: *TRUE-CIRCULAR BARN*

BUILT: 1914
SITE: Millgrove Township
ORIGINAL OWNER:
Morton Friend
BUILDERS: Reynolds, Staley, Compton, Parker, and Bordner
PHOTO: 1985

The Fawn River Farm is home to one of the prettiest round barns in Indiana. It has a magnificent self-supported domed roof and horizontal wood siding. It was built on the side of a hill, which allows easy access to the upper-level hay mow floor. A small silo is located near the center of the barn. The lower level of this 60-foot-diameter bank barn housed cattle.

Sullivan County

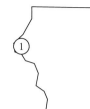

77-1: *TRUE-CIRCULAR BARN*

BUILT: date unknown (razed, 1969)
SITE: Turman Township
ORIGINAL OWNER:
John Thomas
ARCHITECT/BUILDER: unknown
PHOTO: ca. 1970, photographer unknown (Courtesy Audra Rains)

One of three Indiana round barns constructed entirely with poured concrete, this barn was built on a small hill to protect it from the floodwaters of the Wabash River. It was about 60 feet in diameter with one main entry that faced west. The roof was self-supporting, and there was no silo inside.

Switzerland County

78-1: *TRUE-CIRCULAR BARN*

BUILT: 1907
SITE: Posey Township
ORIGINAL OWNER: B. R. Huston
ARCHITECT/BUILDER:
Benton Steele
PHOTO: 1986

This bank barn is one of many designed and built by Benton Steele. Its secluded location in extreme southeast Indiana shows how effective and far-reaching Steele's *Indiana Farmer* advertisements were. Measuring 56 feet in diameter, the barn has a self-supporting, two-pitch gambrel roof with a circular hay track. The hay mow floor is held up by a single center post. A photograph of this barn appeared in the March 13, 1909, issue of the *Indiana Farmer*.

Tippecanoe County

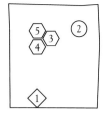

79-1: TWELVE-SIDED BARN

BUILT: date unknown
SITE: Randolph Township
ORIGINAL OWNER: possibly Shoemaker
ARCHITECT/BUILDER: unknown
PHOTO: 1986

Built for sheltering cattle and horses, this 60-foot-diameter barn has a central silo that helps support the roof. The wood-stave silo is held together by metal compression rings and is about 12 feet in diameter.

79-2: TRUE-CIRCULAR BARN

BUILT: ca. 1912 (razed, 1972)
SITE: Fairfield Township

ORIGINAL OWNER: unknown
ARCHITECT/BUILDER: unknown
PHOTO: 1959, George Gould

Little is known about this barn. It had a gable-roofed rectangular entrance, which is common in Indiana round barns. It also had horizontal wood siding and a cupola topped with a metal aerator.

79-3: OCTAGONAL BARN

BUILT: date unknown
SITE: Fairfield Township
ORIGINAL OWNER: unknown
ARCHITECT/BUILDER: unknown
PHOTO: 1970, Gene Worl

This small barn has horizontal wood sides and a metal aerator on top. Little else is known. It is located at 922 South 18th Street in Lafayette.

79-4: OCTAGONAL BARN

BUILT: 1904 (razed, 1970s)
SITE: Wabash Township

ORIGINAL OWNER: Purdue University
ARCHITECT/BUILDER: unknown
PHOTO: date unknown, George Gould

This barn was built on the Purdue University campus in West Lafayette. It was attached to a rectangular cattle barn and was used as a judging pavilion by students. It was 50 feet in diameter, had a poured-concrete floor, and used Professor Franklin King's system of ventilation. It achieved some publicity in "Purdue's New Cattle Barn," *Indiana Farmer*, Dec. 31, 1904, 6.

79-5: OCTAGONAL BARN

BUILT: ca. 1910 (destroyed, date unknown)
SITE: unknown
ORIGINAL OWNER: D. M. Boyle
ARCHITECT/BUILDER: unknown
PHOTO: From an Amatite roofing advertisement, "A Good Roofing Combination, the Boyle Barn, Lafayette, Ind.," *Indiana Farmer*, 1910

This barn was located in the Lafayette area. It consisted of an octagonal barn bound on three sides by a large rectangular structure. Little else is known about the barn.

Tipton County

80-1: TRUE-CIRCULAR BARN

BUILT: 1911–12 (razed, 1973)
SITE: Jefferson Township
ORIGINAL OWNER: Zora A. Watson
BUILDER: Melvin Johnson
PHOTO: 1960, George Gould

As one of three or possibly four round barns built by Melvin Johnson of Kempton, Indiana, this one measured 50 feet across and was constructed with native timber except for its siding. Horses were housed on the east side and cattle on the west. Due to rotting wood, the lower four feet of the horizontal wood siding was replaced with concrete block in the 1960s. A circular eight-foot-diameter cupola once sat on top of the self-supporting, two-pitch gambrel roof.

80-2: TRUE-CIRCULAR BARN

BUILT: date unknown
SITE: Jefferson Township
ORIGINAL OWNER: possibly Charles Parvin
ARCHITECT/BUILDER: unknown
PHOTO: 1986

Measuring 50 feet across, this barn has an east-west driveway through its center. It has horizontal wood siding and a self-supporting, two-pitch gambrel roof.

80-3: TRUE-CIRCULAR BARN

BUILT: ca. 1906
SITE: Cicero Township
ORIGINAL OWNER: Cash Cochran
ARCHITECT/BUILDER: unknown
PHOTO: 1986

An unusual aspect of this barn is that it was built without windows. It is 60 feet in diameter with a north-south driveway and a self-supporting, two-pitch gambrel roof.

80-4: *TRUE-CIRCULAR BARN*

BUILT: 1914 (razed, 1935)

SITE: Prairie Township

ORIGINAL OWNER:
Emmett Harper

BUILDER: Melvin Johnson

PHOTO: not available

This was probably the last of the round barns built by Melvin Johnson. Measuring 75 feet across, it had a central wood-stave silo and a 15-foot-diameter cupola. Except for three feet of concrete blocks, the siding was made of wood.

80-5: *TRUE-CIRCULAR BARN*

BUILT: ca. 1906
(destroyed by fire, 1960s)

SITE: Wildcat Township

ORIGINAL OWNER:
J. W. Morford

ARCHITECT/BUILDER: unknown

PHOTO: From "Round Barn and Silo on Farm of J. W. Morford, Tipton County, Ind.," *Farmer's Guide*, Aug. 11, 1906

This barn was probably built by the same carpenter that built the Cash Cochran barn (#80-3) a few miles to the south. The two barns were nearly identical in appearance. This barn had an east-west driveway.

Union County

81-1: *TRUE-CIRCULAR BARN*

BUILT: 1907

SITE: Center Township

ORIGINAL OWNER:
John Holland

ARCHITECTS/BUILDERS:
probably Benton Steele and Isaac and Emery McNamee

PHOTO: 1985

Originally built for cattle, horses, and hogs, this barn is now used only for hogs. The horse stalls and corn cribs were torn out in 1944. The barn measures 60½ feet in diameter and 51⅓ feet high. There are 21 windows—nine in the lower level and twelve in the upper level. The round cupola is approximately 20 feet in diameter. The original roof was torn off by a tornado and replaced with a three-pitch gambrel roof. It is possible that Benton Steele

designed this barn, since he designed and built one only a few miles away. Isaac McNamee was raised by the John Holland family in nearby Henry County; the owner of this barn may have been a relative.

81-2: *TRUE-CIRCULAR BARN*

BUILT: 1904
(destroyed by fire, pre-1960)

SITE: Brownsville Township

ORIGINAL OWNER:
Oliver LaFuze

ARCHITECT/BUILDER:
Benton Steele

PHOTO: From Louden Machinery Company, "Fitting Up Barns with Louden Hay Tools" (Fairfield, Ia.: 1905)

As word spread that Oliver LaFuze's peers were building round barns, the state legislator decided to build one, too. Benton Steele was hired to design the barn. It was 70 to 80 feet in diameter with a self-supporting, two-pitch gambrel roof. The Louden Machinery Company of Fairfield, Iowa, furnished the circular hay track, and the company featured the barn on the cover of one of its pamphlets.

Vanderburgh County

82-1: *TRUE-CIRCULAR BARN*

BUILT: 1906 (razed, 1980)

SITE: Union Township

ORIGINAL OWNER: Edmond

ARCHITECT/BUILDER:
probably Benton Steele

PHOTO: 1957, Charles Campbell (Courtesy George Gould)

After an August 1905 tornado partially destroyed Edmond's rectangular barn, he consulted the *Indiana Farmer*

before rebuilding. Since there seemed to be a plague of tornadoes those days, the editors recommended round barns. Consequently, Edmond probably contacted Benton Steele to construct the new barn. Measuring 60 feet across with a ramp to the second level, Edmond's new barn satisfied all of his needs. The base consisted of poured concrete 14 inches thick and about 10 feet high to protect it from the floodwaters of the Ohio River. Thick planks of cypress wood, board, and batten were placed above the base. Information on this barn comes from William Gumbert, "Round Barn Built in 1905–06 Seen on Old Henderson Road," newspaper clipping, source and date unknown.

Vermillion County

83-1: TRUE-CIRCULAR BARN

BUILT: 1916
SITE: Eugene Township
ORIGINAL OWNER: O. Earl White
ARCHITECT: O. Earl White
BUILDER: Collett Merriman
PHOTO: 1986

Earl White, a graduate of Purdue University, built this spectacular and aesthetically pleasing bank barn. It is 60 feet high and 60 feet in diameter with 60 windows and a central silo. The vertical wood cypress siding from Louisiana has never been painted and is still in excellent shape. Lumber used as partitions in the barn came from a Newport, Indiana, covered bridge. The lower level housed horses and cattle, grain was stored on the second floor, and hay and straw were stored on the third level. Two ramps provide access to the second floor. The barn was eventually converted to a chicken broiler factory with seven floors, which could hold up to 84,000 chickens at one time. Because of its prominence and location, the barn was used as a landmark for many years by airplane navigators traveling north-south routes between Chicago and Terre Haute, Indiana. A photo and description of this barn appeared in "Big and Round," *Indianapolis News*, July 28, 1975, and in Geraldine Wood, "Round Barn near Quaker Designed and Built in 1916," newspaper clipping, source and date unknown.

Vigo County

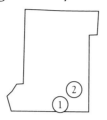

84-1: TRUE-CIRCULAR BARN

BUILT: ca. 1905
SITE: Linton Township
ORIGINAL OWNER: George Bennett
ARCHITECT/BUILDER: unknown
PHOTO: 1985

In 1983, this barn's self-supporting, two-pitch gambrel roof was covered with asphalt at a cost of $7,000. An east-west driveway passes through the barn, and an unusual eight-sided cupola tops the roof.

84-2: TRUE-CIRCULAR BARN

BUILT: 1905
SITE: Pierson Township
ORIGINAL OWNER: Senior
ARCHITECT/BUILDER: unknown
PHOTO: 1985

This unusual barn has a conical roof with four gable-roofed dormers. There is no cupola. An east-west driveway passes through the barn.

Wabash County

85-1: OCTAGONAL BARN

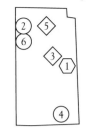

BUILT: ca. 1876–90 (razed, 1990)
SITE: Lagro Township
ORIGINAL OWNER: unknown
ARCHITECT/BUILDER: unknown
PHOTO: 1986

This was probably one of the first round barns constructed in Indiana. Its shape and design were similar to that designed by Elliott Stewart, the man responsible for starting the octagonal barn fad during the 1870s and 1880s. The lower level of this bank barn was constructed with stone in a concrete matrix. Each side was 20 feet long. An octagonal cupola topped the self-supporting roof.

85-2: TRUE-CIRCULAR BARN

BUILT: 1918
SITE: Pleasant Township
ORIGINAL OWNER: Ralph Floor
ARCHITECTS/BUILDERS:
C.V. Kindig and Sons
PHOTO: 1986

Horses were kept on the east and cattle on the west in this 70-foot-diameter barn. When the barn was new, cattle were milked where they stood; later stanchions were added to facilitate the milking process. There was once a concrete feeding area in the center. A single hay track was used to bring hay into the barn. Originally the barn had a cupola, but a tornado blew it off in 1980.

85-3: TEN-SIDED BARN

BUILT: 1901 (razed, 1960s)
SITE: Chester Township
ORIGINAL OWNER: Max Biells
ARCHITECT/BUILDER: unknown
PHOTO: date and photographer unknown (Courtesy Lavonne Grossnickle)

This ten-sided dairy barn had a self-supporting sectional cone roof with no cupola. A silo was located on the northwest side.

85-4: TRUE-CIRCULAR BARN

BUILT: date unknown (razed, 1966)
SITE: Liberty Township
ORIGINAL OWNER: A. C. Roby
ARCHITECT/BUILDER: unknown
PHOTO: not available

This barn had a slate roof, an unusual feature for a true-circular barn. Reportedly, 60 tons of slate were brought to town by rail and transported by wagon to the site. The barn was 60 to 80 feet in diameter with a south entry. The roof required posts for support. Inside there was a circular hay track and a granary on each side of the drive. The hay mow could hold 55 tons of hay. The barn also had vertical wood siding and a round cupola.

85-5: TWELVE-SIDED BARN

BUILT: ca. 1903 (destroyed, date unknown)
SITE: unknown
ORIGINAL OWNER: Levi Kivett
BUILDER: Levi Kivett
PHOTO: From Levi Kivett, "A Circular Round Barn," *Farmer's Guide*, Dec. 5, 1903

An article in a 1903 issue of the *Farmer's Guide* described this barn: "It is built on the duodecimo or twelve-sided plan and is fifty-four feet in diameter, twenty-four feet to the edge of the roof and fourteen feet on each side. It furnishes room for eight head of horses and 32 head of cattle and [has] mow room for nearly one hundred tons of hay and other roughage. . . ." The barn had a central silo and a circular hay track in the self-supporting roof.

85-6: TRUE-CIRCULAR BARN

BUILT: 1911 (razed, date unknown)
SITE: probably PawPaw Township
ORIGINAL OWNER: Jas. M. Early
BUILDER: Jas. M. Early
PHOTO: From Jas. M. Early, "A Round Feeding Barn," *Breeder's Gazette*, Nov. 8, 1911

This barn received publicity in a 1911 issue of the *Breeder's Gazette*. Measuring 100 feet across, this cattle-feeding barn was only surpassed in size by the Frank Littleton barn (#30-2) in Hancock County. It was a bank barn with two ramps leading to the second floor. In the center was a 20-foot-diameter Gurlar-type silo that had a capacity of 65 tons of silage for every 10 feet in height. A gasoline-powered silage cutter was placed on the second-level mow floor because it saved power when the cut silage was raised to fill the silo.

Warren County

86-1: TRUE-CIRCULAR BARN

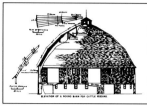

BUILT: ca. 1901 (destroyed, pre-1950)
SITE: unknown
ORIGINAL OWNER: Fremont Goodwine
ARCHITECTS/BUILDERS: Benton Steele and Frank Detraz
PHOTO: From "A Circular Barn with Silo," *Breeder's Gazette*, July 2, 1902

Fremont Goodwine was a state senator and president of the Williamsport National

Bank. In 1901, he heard about round barns through Indianapolis business circles and hired Steele and Detraz to design and construct one on his farm near Williamsport. It measured 80 feet in diameter with a 24-foot-diameter central silo. A self-supporting, three-pitch gambrel roof covered the circular hay track inside. The foundation consisted of poured concrete and concrete block. Its design and construction were featured in a 1902 issue of the *Breeder's Gazette* in one of Steele's first round-barn promotions.

Warrick County

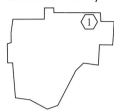

87-1: OCTAGONAL BARN

BUILT: 1898 (razed, 1970s)
SITE: Pigeon Township
ORIGINAL OWNER: Logan Rust
BUILDER: Bill Smith
PHOTO: not available

This 60-foot-diameter barn had a sectional cone roof with a circular hay track and a metal aerator. A north-south driveway passed through the barn.

Washington County

88-1: TRUE-CIRCULAR BARN

BUILT: 1914
SITE: Washington Township
ORIGINAL OWNER: Elmer Williams
BUILDER: Ollie Bowers
PHOTO: 1986

Lebert Williams, son of Elmer, provided the information on this barn. Patterned after the John Hess barn (#36-3) in Jackson County, this barn is 60 feet in diameter with a 12-foot-diameter glazed-tile silo in the center. The barn was built for $735; the silo was an additional $300. Originally the barn had vertical wood siding, but it was replaced with metal siding in 1985.

88-2: FOURTEEN-SIDED BARN

BUILT: 1906
(destroyed by fire, 1988)
SITE: Pierce Township
ORIGINAL OWNER: Grant F. Wright
BUILDERS: Justice Brewer and neighbors
PHOTO: 1986

This 90-foot-diameter horse barn had one main entrance on the south side. Horse stalls encompassed the entire perimeter of the barn. The roof was supported by a large post in the middle and 26 posts in two circular patterns around the center post. Metal sheeting, which replaced a similar covering in 1971, protected the roof. A small five- to six-foot-diameter metal cupola topped the barn.

Wayne County

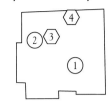

89-1: TRUE-CIRCULAR BARN

BUILT: 1906 (razed, 1969)
SITE: Center Township
ORIGINAL OWNER: Oscar Fulgam
ARCHITECT/BUILDER: Horace Duncan
PHOTO: 1961, George Gould

Oscar Fulgam was the head of the local business college. Horace Duncan and a company from Greenfield, Indiana, built this barn. At 60 feet in diameter with an east-west driveway through the center, the barn was large enough to drive a team and wagon into, turn around, and drive out again. The main entrance consisted of a large rectangular extension from the circular structure. Concrete blocks made up the first floor, and vertical wood siding made up the second floor. In 1928, a tornado tore the roof off, but it was replaced for $2,500 with the one shown in the photograph. The barn was razed in 1969 to make room for the Freedom Missionary Baptist Church.

89-2: *TRUE-CIRCULAR BARN*

BUILT: 1903–04
(destroyed by fire, 1972)
SITE: Jefferson Township
ORIGINAL OWNER:
Wilson Dennis
ARCHITECT: probably Isaac or
Emery McNamee, or
Horace Duncan
BUILDERS: Frank Rhinehart,
Harry Thalls, Ed Raffe, and
Allen Foutz
PHOTO: 1968, Gene Worl

This barn was publicized in many articles by Gene Worl, round-barn and covered-bridge enthusiast. Wilson Dennis was Worl's grandfather. Worl's best account is found in "Round Barns, Covered Bridges and Many Miles in Between," *Hagerstown Exponent*, Apr. 3, 1974. Started in the summer of 1903 and finished in 1904, this 60-foot-diameter barn was painted yellow with red trim. There was no silo inside, but the barn had a self-supporting, two-pitch gambrel roof and a ramp to the hay mow. The idea for the barn came from a similar barn in Henry County. It cost $800 to build.

89-3: *OCTAGONAL BARN*

BUILT: date unknown
SITE: Perry Township
ORIGINAL OWNER:
Harold Oyler
ARCHITECT/BUILDER: unknown
PHOTO: 1985

Used for hogs, this unusual one-story barn is only 30 feet in diameter. Sheet metal covers the roof. The barn is still in use.

89-4: *OCTAGONAL BARN*

BUILT: pre-1900 (razed, 1979)
SITE: Green Township
ORIGINAL OWNER: Shute
ARCHITECT/BUILDER: unknown
PHOTO: date and
photographer unknown
(Courtesy Don Sittloh)

The roof on this barn was very unusual. It was not self-supporting and appeared to be a double-hip roof. There was no central silo or cupola. The barn was originally used for storage.

Wells County

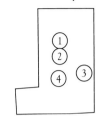

90-1: *TRUE-CIRCULAR BARN*

BUILT: 1911 (razed, 1970s)
SITE: Liberty Township
ORIGINAL OWNER: unknown
ARCHITECT/BUILDER: unknown
PHOTO: 1964, George Gould

Little is known about this barn. The photo shows that it had a two-pitch gambrel roof without a cupola; however, a cupola was probably present at one time. The barn was 50 to 60 feet in diameter and had a main entrance on the east side.

90-2: *TRUE-CIRCULAR BARN*

BUILT: 1910
(roof collapsed, 1988)
SITE: Liberty Township
ORIGINAL OWNER: Tinkle
ARCHITECT/BUILDER: unknown
PHOTO: 1985

Reportedly built by an itinerant carpenter who had built several other round barns, this one was built for $2,000. It was 50 feet in diameter and had vertical wood siding and a round cupola. A rectangular annex was added to the barn at a later date to house a combine.

90-3: *TRUE-CIRCULAR BARN*

BUILT: 1907
SITE: Harrison Township
ORIGINAL OWNER: Loni Dyson
ARCHITECT/BUILDER:
Benton Steele
PHOTO: 1987

When Steele was hired to build this barn, he in turn hired carpenters from the local lum-ber company in Berne to construct it. An excellent photograph showing Steele, the carpenters, and the entire Dyson family posing in front of the newly framed barn is reproduced on page 46 in this book. The barn measures 64 feet across and 50 feet high. It has a three-pitch gambrel roof and a north-south driveway through the center. The barn is known locally as the Dunwiddie round barn.

90-4: *TRUE-CIRCULAR BARN*

BUILT: date unknown
(razed, 1964)
SITE: Chester Township
ORIGINAL OWNER:
Sherman Bell
ARCHITECT/BUILDER: unknown
PHOTO: 1964, George Gould

Originally this barn had a cupola, but it was removed years before the barn was torn down. Measuring 60 feet in diameter, it had a concrete-block foundation, a central driveway, and a self-supporting roof.

White County

91-1: SIXTEEN-SIDED BARN

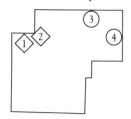

BUILT: 1915
(razed, ca. 1975–85)
SITE: Princeton Township
ORIGINAL OWNER:
Ray "Shorty" Dawson
ARCHITECT: a Wolcott
High School teacher
PHOTO: 1965, George Gould

This unusual barn would have had sixteen sides without the rectangular attachment. With the attachment, the round portion of the barn only had twelve sides. Inside there was a central silo. The circular portion had a two-pitch gambrel roof topped with a small metal aerator.

91-2: SIXTEEN-SIDED BARN

BUILT: 1915 (razed, 1985)
SITE: Princeton Township
ORIGINAL OWNER: Covington
ARCHITECT: a Wolcott
High School teacher
PHOTO: 1965, George Gould

Constructed along the same lines as the Dawson barn (#91-1), this barn would have had sixteen sides without the rectangular attachment. Unlike the Dawson barn, this one only had eight sides without the addition because the circular portion encompassed 180 degrees, or a half circle. The barn's two-pitch sectional roof never had a cupola or an aerator. There was no silo in the barn.

91-3: TRUE-CIRCULAR BARN

BUILT: 1906
SITE: Liberty Township
ORIGINAL OWNER:
Elizabeth Kitchen
ARCHITECT: Benton Steele
BUILDER: James Malone
PHOTO: 1962, George Gould

Elizabeth Kitchen's round barn was designed after the Floyd Whetsal barn (#29-3) in Hamilton County. It is one of three round barns in Indiana known to still have the original blueprints. Of additional historical value is the correspondence between Kitchen and Benton Steele and Horace Duncan. Kitchen obtained the idea from an advertisement in the *Indiana Farmer* and contacted Steele to supply the blueprints for the barn. Steele sent a set of four plans, a lumber bill, and carpenter's specifications that would allow any competent carpenter to build it without further assistance from Steele. It is not known how many barns were sold by Steele in this manner, but based on the number of similar-looking barns in Indiana and the surrounding states, the number could be tremen-

dous. The barn measures 60 feet across and 20 feet to the eaves. It has "a finely cemented floor, a six barrel water tank, a driveway through the center with great sliding doors, a corn crib, two granaries, eight stalls for horses, 16 stanchions for cattle [and] convenient roomy halls for feeding stock." In 1911, Horace Duncan wrote Kitchen claiming an infringement on his patent. Duncan was asking for $25 in fees to buy the right to the patent or he would place the matter in the hands of his attorney. Steele's response to Kitchen was to ignore Duncan and forget the matter, which is what she apparently did. Mary Hacker of Buffalo, Indiana, provided most of the information on this barn.

91-4: TRUE-CIRCULAR BARN

BUILT: date unknown
(razed, pre-1940)
SITE: Cass Township
ORIGINAL OWNER: unknown
ARCHITECT/BUILDER: unknown
PHOTO: not available

According to neighbors, a round barn used to stand in extreme eastern White County. It had vertical siding and an east-west driveway through the center. Little else is known about the barn.

Notes

Preface

1. George E. Gould, "The Round Barn Fad," *Outdoor Indiana*, (Indiana Department of Natural Resources), November 1980, 5–11.

2. Wilson L. Wells, *Barns in the U.S.A.* (San Diego, Calif.: Acme Printing Co., 1976). Lowell J. Soike, *Without Right Angles: The Round Barns of Iowa* (Des Moines, Iowa: Iowa State Historical Department, Office of Historic Preservation, 1983).

A Round Indiana

1. Thanks to Lowell J. Soike, Iowa State Historical Department; Keith A. Sculle, Illinois Historic Preservation Agency; and Timothy L. Ericson, Milwaukee Urban Archives, University of Wisconsin, Milwaukee, for providing me with these figures. A comprehensive study of round barns in Wisconsin might reveal more barns in that state than in Indiana.

2. Soike, *Without Right Angles* (cited above), 4; and H. Wayne Price and Keith A. Sculle, "The Failed Round Barn Experiment: Horace Duncan's Experience as a Carpenter," *Pioneer American Society Transactions*, vol. 6 (1983): 1–6.

3. Ernest A. Wilkinson, "Hoosier Prairie: Some of the Best Cropland in the World," *Indianapolis Star*, Mar. 17, 1986, 2C.

4. Ibid.

5. If known, the proper name assigned to a barn is the name of the original owner.

6. In a book by Samuel Chamberlain, *Domestic Architecture in Rural France* (New York: Architectural Book Publishing Co., ca. 1928; New York: Publishers Group West, Hastings House, 1981), a drawing of an octagonal barn with a thatch roof is shown (plate 21, "Barns of Normandy"). Details on its construction are not known.

7. Soike, *Without Right Angles* (cited above), 5. Also, Paul Leland Hawarth, *George Washington: Farmer* (Indianapolis: Bobbs-Merrill Company, 1915), 124–25.

8. Eric Arthur and Dudley Witney, *The Barn: A Vanishing Landmark in North America* (Greenwich, Conn.: New York Graphic Society, 1972), 147–57. Used by permission of the Canadian Publishers, McClelland & Stewart, Toronto.

9. According to *Webster's Biographical Dictionary* (Springfield, Mass.: G.&C. Merriam Company, 1959), Franz Joseph Gall (1758–1828) was a German physician and founder of phrenology. Gall studied the brains and skulls of men and animals and sought to establish a relationship between mental faculties and the size and shape of the skull.

10. Soike, *Without Right Angles* (cited above), 6.

11. Carl F. Schmidt, *The Octagon Fad* (Scottsville, N.Y.: privately printed, 1958), 1.

12. According to Soike in *Without Right Angles*, 6, "farm journals had ceased any mention of Fowler by the early 1860s."

13. J. Estes Ratcliff, "The Round Barn Is No More," *Henry County* (Ind.) *Historicalog*, fall 1974.

14. Soike, *Without Right Angles* (cited above), 10. According to Soike, Stewart's plan appeared in two 1874–75 winter issues of the Buffalo, N.Y., *Live-Stock Journal*. Elliott W. Stewart's "An Octagonal Barn" was also reprinted as a series in the Chicago *National Live-Stock Journal 9*, (Feb., Mar., and Apr. 1878): 52–53, 100–101, 149.

15. In *Without Right Angles* (cited above), Soike was the first to name the barn construction period between 1870 and 1900 as the "Octagon Era."

16. All of these advantages were cited in Elliott W. Stewart, *Feeding Animals: A Practical Work upon the Laws of Animal Growth Specially Applied to the Breeding and Rearing of Horses, Cattle, Dairy Cows, Sheep and Swine*, 2d ed. (Lake View, N.Y.: privately printed, 1883), 89–92.

17. Stewart's octagonal plan appeared in *Cultivator and Country Gentleman* 41, Aug. 31, 1876, 554; *American Agriculturalist* 35 (July 1876), 258–59; "Construction of Barns," *Illustrated Annual Register of Rural Affairs* (Albany, N.Y.: *Cultivator and Country Gentleman*, 1878), 229, 249–52; and J. P. Sheldon, *Dairy Farming* (London and New York: Cassell, Petter, Gilpin and Company, ca. 1885).

18. "Octagonal Barns," *Cultivator and Country Gentleman* 49 (Aug. 14, 1884), 579.

19. For more information, see barn entries #22-1 (Floyd County), #39-2 (Jefferson County), and #85-1 (Wabash County) in the "Catalog of Round Barns."

20. Ratcliff, "The Round Barn Is No More" (cited above).

21. William G. Hope, "Door Prairie Barn" (poster), (LaPorte, Ind.: privately printed, ca. 1980).

22. Ibid.

23. Charlotte Bass, "Historical Landmark Round Barn," *LaPorte Herald-Argus*, Apr. 11, 1980.

24. Hope, "Door Prairie Barn" (cited above).

The Ideal Circular Barn

1. Franklin H. King, "The Construction of Silos," Bulletin 28 (Madison, Wis.: University of Wisconsin Agricultural Experiment Station, 1891).

2. Franklin H. King, "Plan of a Barn for a Dairy Farm," Seventh Annual Report (Madison, Wis.: University of Wisconsin Agricultural Experiment Station, 1890). As described by Roger L. Welsch in "Nebraska's Round Barns," *Nebraska History* 51 (1970), 51, balloon-frame construction is "a form of framing in which the weight of the roof and upper floors is borne by a series of closely spaced light weight, upright studs, each linking the plate and the first floor sill. Almost all modern frame buildings are of balloon construction, the roof being carried by vertical two-by-fours in the walls."

3. The plan appeared in Franklin H. King, "Plan of a Barn for a Dairy Farm" (cited above), 183; *Hoard's Dairyman*, Apr. 19, 1895 and Mar. 26, 1897; J. H. Sanders, *Practical Hints about Farm Building* (Chicago: J. H. Sanders Publishing Co., 1893), 100–101; *Breeder's Gazette*, Apr. 7, 1897); *Farm Buildings* (Chicago: *Breeder's Gazette*, 1916), 126, 129; and Franklin H. King, *A Text Book of the Physics of Agriculture*, 6th ed. (Madison, Wis.: Franklin H. King, 1914), 341–42.

4. See barn entries #48-7 (Henry Kemp barn) and #61-4 (W. H. York barn) in the "Catalog of Round Barns" for more information.

5. Joseph E. Wing, "A Quaker Settlement in Indiana," *Breeder's Gazette*, Sept. 7, 1910, 392–93.

6. Circular barns were referred to by many different names, such as a cylindrical barn, round barn, cyclone barn, barrel barn, and silo barn. A silo barn is simply a barn with a silo in its center.

7. William Hill, "The Silo and Silage," *Breeder's Gazette*, July 29, 1903, 168.

8. Dorthea Riley, granddaughter of Emery McNamee, interview with author, 1988. Also, the 1870 and 1880 Bureau of Census records list Isaac and Emery McNamee as carpenters.

9. Linda J. Harsin, "Facts about Benton Steele" (unpublished outline). Linda J. Harsin, granddaughter of Benton Steele, letter to Lowell Soike, Aug. 8, 1911. Also, Shirley Koch, granddaughter of Benton Steele, telephone interview with author, 1988. In Steele's own publication—*Ideal Circular Barn* (Pendleton, Ind.: privately printed, ca. 1905), 2—Steele claims to have been in the barn planning, designing, and building business for fifteen years. From 1902 to 1909, Steele advertised his plans in many issues of *Indiana Farmer* and occasionally promoted the circular barn in *Hoard's Dairyman* and *Farmer's Guide*.

10. Thanks to Shirley Koch, granddaughter of Benton Steele, for providing me with the text of this note.

11. Justin E. Walsh, Allen F. January, Elizabeth Shanahan, Vincent A. Giroux, Jr., *A Biographical Directory of the Indiana General Assembly*, vol. 2, 1900–1984 (Indianapolis: Select Committee on the Centennial History of the Indiana General Assembly, in cooperation with the Indiana Historical Bureau, 1984), 157.

12. "A Circular Barn with Silo," *Breeder's Gazette*, July 2, 1902, 43–44.

13. Wymond J. Beckett, letter to Samuel "Frank" Detraz and Benton Steele, Feb. 20, 1902. Reprinted in Benton Steele, *Ideal Circular Barn* (Pendleton, Ind.: privately printed, ca. 1905), 3.

14. Samuel "Frank" Detraz and Benton Steele, "Round Barn for Ranchmen," *Breeder's Gazette*, Mar. 4, 1903, 424–25.

15. Benton Steele's address shown in *Indiana Farmer* and *Breeder's Gazette* articles indicate he moved to Pendleton sometime between July 20, 1902, and February 14, 1903. Emery McNamee's address is listed in the *Anderson Morning Herald*, Feb. 20, 1903, 5. Isaac McNamee's age kept him from traveling much. Most of the circular barns directly attributed to him are located within forty miles of Knightstown. He often took on small jobs. For example, he built ". . . a very handsome veranda at [the] home of John T. Girty on East Main St." in Knightstown (*Knightstown Banner*, Sept. 2, 1904, 5). Emery, on the other hand, accepted jobs that

took him far away. In 1908, he was working in the area of Taylor and Grant counties in Iowa and built a round barn for a man named Reid; and in 1913, he built at least one round barn in Saskatchewan, Canada. He later settled in Roundup, Montana, but he moved back to Indiana in the 1920s (Helen McNamee Barney, niece of Emery McNamee, interview with author, 1988; see also, Emery McNamee, "A Round Barn," *Breeder's Gazette*, Jan. 5, 1910).

16. "A Circular Barn with Silo," *Breeder's Gazette*, July 2, 1902, 43–44.

17. In 1902, Horace Duncan was sent to Artis, South Dakota, to build a large round barn for F. W. Boettcher, a bank president and wealthy farmer. By mid-1903, Duncan, Steele, the McNamees, and Detraz had constructed a circular barn with a self-supporting roof for owners by the name of Stow and Gingrich near Hamburg, Iowa. Steele, *Ideal Circular Barn* (cited above), 3.

18. "A Circular Barn with Silo," *Breeder's Gazette*, July 2, 1902, 43–44.

19. Samuel "Frank" Detraz and Benton Steele, "The Circular Ideal Barn," *Indiana Farmer*, Feb. 14, 1903, 1.

20. Steele, *Ideal Circular Barn* (cited above), 3.

21. This storm made front-page headlines in many regional newspapers, including the June 25, 1902, issues of the *Indianapolis Star* and *Anderson Morning Herald*.

22. "Cyclone Proof: Cyclones Have No Disastrous Effect on Cylindrical Barns," *Anderson Morning Herald*, Feb. 20, 1903, 3.

23. Phyllis Kingen, operator of the former Littleton farm, interview with author, January 1988. The Kingen family has operated the farm since 1911.

24. Benton Steele, "A Circular Barn," *Indiana Farmer*, Jan. 9, 1904, 1.

25. The American Biographical Society, *Indianapolis Men of Affairs* (Indianapolis, Ind.: Paul Donald Brown, 1923), 388–89.

26. Isaac S. McNamee, Horace Duncan, and Frank L. Littleton, inventors, "Self-supporting Conical Roof," U.S. patent no. 804,427. The patent application was filed on December 13, 1904, and given on November 14, 1905. The term "conical" was commonly used for a roof during this period even though it was not a true cone. "Bowl" or "dome" would have been more accurate. In today's terminology, the correct language is a two-pitch gambrel roof.

27. Although it is not documented, it is likely that Detraz and Steele would have contacted the local universities first, then gone elsewhere. C. B. Dorsey's visit was mentioned in "A Revelation to Him," *Pendleton Republican*, May 1903, in Steele, *Ideal Circular Barn* (cited above); Steele, *Ideal Circular Barn*, 3; and Steele, "Many Silos To Be Built," *Indiana Farmer*, May 9, 1903, 9. During the visit, Steele

apparently showed Dorsey the John W. Whisler barn in Hancock County, the William Hill barn in Rush County, and the Jim Sears barn in Madison County as well as the silos on the Parker brothers' farm in Henry County.

28. Illinois Farmer's Institute, "A Round Dairy Barn," *Breeder's Gazette*, Nov. 2, 1910, 946. It is likely that Horace Duncan was the carpenter, but it could also have been Emery McNamee or Benton Steele.

29. Wilber J. Fraser, "Economy of the Round Barn," Bulletin 143 (Urbana, Ill.: University of Illinois Agricultural Experiment Station, Feb. 1910).

30. H. Wayne Price and Keith A. Sculle, "The Failed Round Barn Experiment: Horace Duncan's Experience as a Carpenter," *Pioneer American Society Transactions*, vol. 6, 1983, 3.

31. "Build the Farm Barn Large Enough for Future Needs; It Should be Well Lighted and Ventilated," *Farmer's Guide*, Aug. 12, 1916, 5.

32. Benton Steele, "A Circular Barn," *Indiana Farmer*, Jan. 9, 1904, 1.

33. Duncan charged $10.00 for the farm rights to build a circular barn. If rights included blueprints, then Duncan charged based on the barn's size. Including farm rights, a 40-foot-diameter barn cost $10.00; a 60-foot-diameter barn, $22.60; an 80-foot-diameter barn, $40.20; and a 90- to 110-foot-diameter barn, $50.00. From Horace Duncan's brochure, "Duncan's Type of Barn" (Knightstown, Ind.: privately printed, ca. 1910).

34. Mrs. Walter Norris and Dorthea Riley, relatives of Emery McNamee, interview with author, 1988.

35. Steele's last known promotion in the *Indiana Farmer* was an article submitted by Thomas Singleton, a farmer who built a circular barn from plans that Steele had sent him (Thomas Singleton, "Livestock Round Barn," *Indiana Farmer*, June 5, 1909, 1). Kansas was a logical destination for Steele because his mother, brothers, and sisters had been living there since Steele was fourteen years old, when he had stayed in Indiana to work as a carpenter's apprentice in the Willow Springs–Warrington area (Shirley Koch, granddaughter of Benton Steele, telephone interview with author, 1988).

36. It was Steele's practice was to send a set of circular-barn blueprints and building instructions to buyers. It was then up to the farmer to hire a competent carpenter to carry out the plans. In his article "The Round Barn," published in the November 30, 1907, issue of the *Indiana Farmer*, he explained some of his frustrations with carpenters: "The greatest difficulty I have had to overcome has been with mechanics who . . . are universally opposed to circular construction, until convinced of its simplicity and [ease] of its construction. It is noteworthy, however, that when

once a carpenter has worked on circular construction, he prefers it to any other style."

37. "A Novel and Beautiful Barn," *Monticello Herald*, July 19, 1906, 1. Kitchen probably learned of the round barn from Benton Steele, "Circular Barn for Forty to Eighty Acre Farm," *Indiana Farmer*, Dec. 30, 1905, 1.

38. Horace Duncan, letter to Elizabeth Kitchen, Jan. 24, 1911.

39. Benton Steele, letter to Elizabeth Kitchen, Jan. 28, 1911.

40. Price and Sculle, "The Failed Round Barn Experiment" (cited above), 3.

41. In 1918, a man believed to be Horace Duncan contacted Albert Aikens, owner of a round barn in Carroll County, and claimed a patent infringement. Aikens paid the man eighty-five dollars. See barn entry #08-1 in the "Catalog of Round Barns" for additional information on the barn.

42. Shirley Willard, ed., "Kindig Builders," in *Fulton County Folks*, vol. 1. (Marceline, Mo.: Walsworth Publishing Co., 1974), 85–87.

43. Ibid.

44. Purdue University professors apparently taught their students about circular-barn construction because several barns in Indiana were built by graduates of Purdue who claimed they learned about it in a class at Purdue.

45. Lynn Robertson, "Farm Buildings in Relationship to Farm Management in Indiana," Bulletin 435 (West Lafayette, Ind.: Purdue University Agricultural Experiment Station, March 1939), 13.

Catalog of Round Barns

1. I compiled this catalog from numerous sources, particularly from the unpublished notes of round-barn enthusiasts Gene Worl and George Gould and passages from Wilson Wells's *Barns in the U.S.A.* (all cited above). Current owners and relatives of the original owners of the barns also provided some of the details. Additional sources include newspaper clippings, agricultural bulletins, and surveys conducted by others.

Sources

Altman and Clymer. "A Round Barn." *Indiana Farmer*, Mar. 1, 1902.

American Biographical Society. *Indianapolis Men of Affairs* (Indianapolis, Ind.: Paul Donald Brown, 1923).

Anderson, George. "Practical Barn Plans." *Farmer's Guide*, Apr. 8, 1911.

Arthur, Eric, and Dudley Witney. *The Barn: A Vanishing Landmark in North America.* Greenwich, Conn.: New York Graphic Society, 1972.

Bass, Charlotte. "Historical Landmark Round Barn." *LaPorte Herald-Argus*, Apr. 11, 1980.

Baute, Betty. "Round Barns of Jackson County." *Watt High Lights* (Jackson County Rural Electric), vol. 41, no. 5 (Oct. 1986).

"Big and Round." *Indianapolis News*, July 28, 1975.

"A Big Round Barn." *Farmer's Guide*, Sept. 6, 1913.

Birchfield, Rodger. "County's Last Round Barn To Be Eatery." Newspaper clipping, source and date unknown.

Breeder's Gazette. Chicago. 1895–1910.

Brown, Andreas, and Hal Morgan. *Prairie Fires and Pale Moons: The American Photographic Postcard, 1900–1920* (Boston: David R. Godine, 1981).

Brown, Tim. "Fog Tones." *LaPorte Herald-Argus*, Feb. 21, 1981.

Brown, Tim, and Jeff Place. "A Glimpse of Falls Past." *LaPorte Herald-Argus*, Sept. 28, 1982.

"Build the Farm Barn Large Enough for Future Needs; It Should Be Well Lighted and Ventilated." *Farmer's Guide*, Aug. 12, 1916.

"Burning of Round Barn Destroys Unusual Dalton Pike Landmark." *Hagerstown Exponent*, Feb. 11, 1971.

Burt, S. C. "Advantages and Disadvantages of the Round Barn: First One Built 25 Years Ago." *Indiana Farmer's Guide*, Nov. 9, 1918.

Cavinder, Fred D. "Barn in the Round." *Indianapolis Star Magazine*, Oct. 22, 1961.

"A Circular Barn with Silo." *Breeder's Gazette*, July 9, 1902.

"Concrete Barn on the Farm of M. S. Yoder, LaGrange County." *Indiana Farmer*, Mar. 26, 1910.

Cox, Maxine. "Round Barn Restoration Includes 'Spot' for Crafts." Newspaper clipping, source and date unknown.

Cultivator and Country Gentleman. Albany, N.Y. 1854–1930.

"Cyclone Proof: Cyclones Have No Disastrous Effect on Cylindrical Barns." *Anderson Morning Herald*, Feb. 20, 1903.

Davis, C. B. "A Good Round Barn." *Indiana Farmer*, Apr. 14, 1906.

Detraz, Samuel "Frank," and Benton Steele. "The Circular Ideal Barn." *Indiana Farmer*, Feb. 14, 1903.

———. "Round Barn for Ranchmen." *Breeder's Gazette*, Mar. 4, 1903.

Doolittle, Fran. "Round Barns in Retrospect." *Outdoor Indiana*, Oct. 1973.

Duncan, Horace. *Duncan's Type of Barn*. Knightstown, Ind.: privately printed, ca. 1910.

Early, Jas. M. "A Round Feeding Barn." *Breeder's Gazette*, Nov. 8, 1911.

Ebklaw, K. J. T. *Farm Structures*. New York: Macmillan Co., 1916.

Echterling, Edward. "Practical Round Barns." *Farmer's Guide*, May 18, 1912.

Edwards, C. B. "Two Barns of Unique Design." *Country Life*, Oct. 1, 1911.

Englehart, Gordon. "Barns in the Round." *Louisville Courier-Journal*, Oct. 23, 1966.

Evans, Tim. "Round Barns Still Lure Oddity Seekers." *Columbus* (Ind.) *Republic*, May 18, 1982.

"Famous Old 'Round Barn' Undergoing Demolition." *Richmond Graphic*, Feb. 2, 1969.

"Farm Barns." *Farmer's Guide*, Jan. 23, 1915.

Farm Buildings. Chicago: *Breeder's Gazette*, 1913.

Farmer's Guide. Huntington, Ind. 1902–18.

"Festival in the Round." *Indianapolis Star Magazine*, June 27, 1971.

"Fire Razes Round Barn." *Richmond Palladium-Item* and *Richmond Sun-Telegram*, Feb. 11, 1971.

"Fitting Up Barns with Louden Hay Tools." Fairfield, Ia.: Louden Machinery Company, 1905.

Foster, W. A. *Farm Buildings*. New York: John Wiley and Sons, Inc., 1922.

Fraser, Wilber J. "Economy of the Round Dairy Barn," Bulletin 143 (Urbana, Ill.: University of Illinois Agricultural Experiment Station, Feb. 1910)

———. "The Round Barn," Circular 230, revision of Bulletin 143 (Urbana, Ill.: University of Illinois Agricultural Experiment Station, Sept. 1918).

"A Good Roofing Combination, The Boyle Barn, Lafayette, Ind." *Indiana Farmer*, 1910.

"A Good Round Barn." *Indiana Farmer*, Oct. 5, 1907.

Gould, George E. "The Round Barn Fad." *Outdoor Indiana*, Nov. 1980.

———. "Round Barns of Indiana." West Lafayette, Ind.: 1980. Unpublished catalog.

Gumbert, William. "Round Barn Built in 1905–06 Seen on Old Henderson Road." Newspaper clipping, source and date unknown.

Hawarth, Paul Leland. *George Washington: Farmer*. Indianapolis: Bobbs-Merrill Company, 1915.

"Heard Round Barn to be Saved." *Eastern Indiana Farmer*, vol. 17, no. 9, Apr. 6, 1973.

"Henry County's Last Round Barn Victim of Last Week's Snowstorm." *Richmond Palladium-Item*, Dec. 26, 1973.

Hiigli, Mary. "Six-Sided Barn Now 87 Years Old." *LaPorte Herald-Argus*, Dec. 2, 1967.

Hill, William. "The Silo and Silage." *Breeder's Gazette*, July 29, 1903.

"History on Wheels Summer Tour." Cedar Lake Summer Fest–Wander Indiana 1985. Cedar Lake Historical Association, Cedar Lake Chamber of Commerce, 1985.

Hoard's Dairyman. Ft. Atkinson, Wis. 1891–1920.

Hoffman, Jim. "Barn is 58, Builder is 93." *Louisville Times*, Nov. 29, 1966.

Hood, Doris. *Fulton County's Round Barns*. Rochester, Ind.: privately printed, July 1971.

Hope, William G. "Door Prairie Barn" (poster). LaPorte, Ind.: privately printed, ca. 1980.

Illinois Farmer's Institute. "A Round Dairy Barn." *Breeder's Gazette*, Nov. 2, 1910.

"Important Things to Remember in Planning a New Barn." *Farmer's Guide*, Aug. 18, 1917.

Indiana Farmer. Indianapolis. 1875–1918.

"Interior of a Modern Dairy Stable on Farm of D. C. Slipher, Clinton County, Indiana," *Farmer's Guide*, Sept. 15, 1917.

Jost, Larry. *The Round and Five-or-More-Equal-Sided Barns of Wisconsin*. Waukesha, Wis.: privately printed, 1980.

King, Franklin H. "The Construction of Silos," Bulletin 28. Madison, Wis.: University of Wisconsin Agricultural Experiment Station, 1891.

———. "Plan of a Barn for a Dairy Farm." *Seventh Annual Report*. Madison, Wis.: University of Wisconsin Agricultural Experiment Station, 1890.

———. *A Text Book of the Physics of Agriculture*, 6th ed. Madison, Wis.: Franklin H. King, 1914.

Kivett, Levi. "A Circular Barn." *Farmer's Guide*, Dec. 5, 1903.

Knight, Max. "Large Round Barn in Center Township May Be Lost by Zoning." *Richmond Palladium-Item*, Oct. 21, 1964.

Knight, Max. "Randolph County Has Five Round Barns." *Richmond Palladium-Item*, Nov. 28, 1972.

"Landmarks for Travelers." *Richmond Palladium-Item*, Mar. 1936.

Lord, Fred S. "Round Barn Constructed in 1906 West of City Gave Road Its Name." *Richmond Palladium-Item*, Jan. 27, 1957.

McGeady, Michael E. "A Project for the Historical American Buildings Survey: The Round House, Jay County Fair Grounds, Portland, Indiana." Arch. 221, Historic American Buildings Survey I. Muncie, Ind.: Drawings and Documents Archive, College of Architecture and Planning, Ball State University, Nov. 10, 1982.

McNamee, Emery. "A Round Barn." *Breeder's Gazette*, Jan. 5, 1910.

"Money Saving Round Barn." *Farmer's Guide*, Feb. 10, 1912.

National Live-Stock Journal. Chicago. 1872–88.

"A Novel and Beautiful Barn." *Monticello Herald*, July 19, 1906.

Oates, William A. "Indiana Round Barns, Unique in Farm History." *Indianapolis Star*, ca. 1972.

"An Octagonal Barn." *Farmer's Guide*, date unknown.

Painter, Anna Mercy. *A Homespun Quaker Family Chronicle: A Story of Hoosier Home Life One Hundred Years Ago*. Niagra, N.Y.: Niagara Frontier Press, 1970.

Parker, Sam. "Round Barn May Be Around." *Columbus* (Ind.) *Republic*, Feb. 10, 1973.

Peters, Mrs. Kyle. "Back When." Newspaper clipping, source and date unknown.

Pinchon, L. A. "Alfalfa Growing Adds to Livestock Feeder's Profits, Is Important Crop on Smith Farm." *Farmer's Guide*, Sept. 25, 1915.

Porter, Marcia C. "Painting Project." *LaPorte Herald-Argus*, June 15, 1983.

Price, H. Wayne, and Keith A. Sculle. "The Failed Round Barn Experiment: Horace Duncan's Experience as a Carpenter." *Pioneer American Society Transactions*, vol. 6, 1983.

"Purdue's New Cattle Barn." *Indiana Farmer*, Dec. 31, 1904.

Ratcliff, J. Estes. "The Round Barn Is No More." *Henry County* (Ind.) *Historicalog*, fall issue, 1974.

"A Revelation to Him," *Pendleton Republican*, May 1903. In Benton Steele, *Ideal Circular Barn*. Pendleton, Ind.: privately printed, ca. 1905.

Robertson, Lynn. "Farm Buildings in Relationship to Farm Management in Indiana," Bulletin 435. West Lafayette, Ind.: Purdue University Agricultural Experiment Station, March 1939.

"Round Barn and Silo on Farm of J. W. Morford, Tipton County, Ind." *Farmer's Guide*, Aug. 11, 1906.

"Round Barn in Owen County." *Owen Leader*, Feb. 20, 1986.

"Round Barn of W. J. Beckett, Dearborn County, Ind." *Indiana Farmer*, Dec. 22, 1906.

"Round Barn on Farm of H. E. Clevenger, Randolph County." *Indiana Farmer*, Oct. 6, 1906.

"Round Barns." *Indiana Farmer*, Mar. 13, 1909.

"Round Barns." *Indiana Farmer*, May 14, 1910.

"Round Barns, Covered Bridges and Many Miles in Between." *Hagerstown Exponent*, Apr. 3, 1974.

"Round Barns, Covered Bridges Interest 2 Indiana Buffs." *Tri-State Trader*, vol. 7, no. 10, June 15, 1974.

Salzarulo, Frank. "39 Year Old Round Barn Ideal for Dairy Use." *Indianapolis News*, 1948.

"Save Barn Campaign Under Way." *Columbus* (Ind.) *Republic*, Aug. 1, 1973.

Schmidt, Carl F. *The Octagon Fad*. Scottsville, N.Y.: privately printed, 1958.

Schulz, Robert C. "An Overview of American Barns," Arch. 321, Historic American Buildings Survey II. Muncie, Ind.: Drawings and Documents Archive, College of Architecture and Planning, Ball State University, Spring 1984.

———. "Round Barn: Rural Route 1, Parker, Box 351, Windsor Road, Stoney Creek Township, Randolph County, Exterior Description," Arch. 221, Historic American Buildings Survey I. Muncie, Ind.: Drawings and Documents Archive, College of Architecture and Planning, Ball State University, Nov. 2, 1983.

"Silo and Barn Combined." *Indiana Farmer*, Feb. 24, 1906.

Simons, Richard S. "The Best of Both Barns." *Indianapolis Star Magazine*, Sept. 18, 1977.

Singleton, Thomas. "Livestock Round Barn." *Indiana Farmer*, June 5, 1909.

Slaughter, Kathy. "Well-Rounded Barn Helps To Cut Corners." *Frankfort Times*, Oct. 14, 1985.

Sloane, Eric. *An Age of Barns*. New York: Random House, Inc., Ballantine Books, 1974.

Smith, Leveda. "County's Round Barn Is Well Preserved." *Monticello Daily Herald-Journal*, May 1, 1976.

———. "Seeing Unusual? Round Barn Fills Bill." *Lafayette Journal and Courier*, Nov. 18, 1979.

Snyder, S. C. "A Remodeled Barn." *Farmer's Guide*, July 11, 1908.

Snyder, Vicki. "Schaeffer Farm, An Unusual Landmark." *Cedar Lake Register*, May 5, 1976.

Soike, Lowell J. *Without Right Angles: The Round Barns of Iowa*. Des Moines, Ia.: Iowa State Historical Department, Office of Historic Preservation, 1983.

"Stand in the Corner?" *Vincennes Sun-Commercial*, Jan. 19, 1986.

Stark, Ralph W. "No Corners Found in Barn That's Round." *Boone, Your County Magazine*, vol. 1, no. 4, May 1974, 10.

Starr, Mary Agnes. "Round Barn West of City To Be Razed; Baptist Church Will Replace Landmark." *Richmond Palladium-Item*, Feb. 26, 1969.

Steele, Benton. "A Circular Barn." *Indiana Farmer*, Jan. 9, 1904.

———. "Circular Barn for Forty to Eighty Acre Farm." *Indiana Farmer*, Dec. 30, 1905.

———. "A Complete Feeding Barn." *Indiana Farmer*, Mar. 15, 1902.

———. "Farm Dairy Barn." *Indiana Farmer*, Jan. 14, 1905.

———. "Grouping, Planning and General Arrangement of Farm Buildings." *Indiana Farmer*, Apr. 9, 1904.

———. *Ideal Circular Barn*. Pendleton, Ind.: privately printed, ca. 1905.

———. "Many Silos To Be Built." *Indiana Farmer*, May 9, 1903.

———. "New Type of Circular Barn." *In Farm Buildings*. Chicago: *Breeder's Gazette*, 1913.

———. "A Round Barn." *Indiana Farmer*, Sept. 5, 1908.

———. "The Round Barn." *Indiana Farmer*, Nov. 30, 1907.

———. "A Round Dairy Barn." *Hoard's Dairyman*, Apr. 3, 1908.

———. "Silo Plans." *Indiana Farmer*, Dec. 28, 1907.

———. "Two Barns Compared." *Indiana Farmer*, Dec. 15, 1906.

Stewart, Elliott W. *Feeding Animals: A Practical Work upon the Laws of Animal Growth Specially Applied to the Rearing and Feeding of Horses, Cattle, Dairy Cows, Sheep and Swine*. 2d ed. Lake View, N.Y.: privately printed, 1883.

Strohm, Paul E. "Round Barns: A Species Threatened by Extension—The George Hall Barn, Jackson County, Indiana: A Case Study." Arch. 430. Muncie, Ind.: Drawings and Documents Archive, College of Architecture and Planning, Ball State University, Apr. 28, 1980.

Stuckwish, Melissa. "Until One Burned, Stuckwish Farm Had Unique Pair of Barns." *Brownstown Banner*, Feb. 1, 1984.

"$10 for Round Barn: But Where Can It Be Moved?" *Tri-State Trader*, Mar. 16, 1974.

"Ten Thousand Dollars a Year from Barred Rocks: A Profitable Venture in Poultry." *Farmer's Guide*, Mar. 20, 1915.

Thomas, Bill. "His Round Barn Is Masterpiece, Owner Says Proudly." (Dearborn County, Ind.) *Enquirer*, date unknown.

"A Twelve Sided Barn." *Farmer's Guide*, May 30, 1914.

"Unique Grant County Farm Barns Go Round and Round." *Marion Chronicle-Tribune*, Jan. 28, 1962.

Wallace's Farmer. Des Moines, Ia. 1893–1930.

Walters, H. Max. "Fayette County's Round Barn Attracts Widespread Attention." *Connersville News-Examiner*, date unknown.

Welsch, Roger L. "Nebraska's Round Barns." *Nebraska History* 51 (1970).

Wells, Wilson L. *Barns in the U.S.A.* San Diego, Calif.: Acme Printing Co., 1976.

Wilkinson, Ernest A. "Hoosier Prairie: Some of the Best Cropland in the World." *Indianapolis Star*, Mar. 17, 1986.

Willard, Shirley, ed. "Kindig Builders." In *Fulton County Folks*, Vol. 1. Marceline, Mo.: Walsworth Publishing Co., 1974.

Williams, Bryan B. "A Round Barn." *Farmer's Guide*, Aug. 23, 1913.

Wing, Joseph E. "A Quaker Settlement in Indiana." *Breeder's Gazette*, Sept. 7, 1910.

Wood, Geraldine. "Round Barn near Quaker Designed and Built in 1916." Newspaper clipping, source and date unknown.

Wood, Henry. "Beauty in Barns." *Indianapolis Star*, Jan. 18, 1953.

Wood, Henry S. "Cadillac of Barns: Round Barn Found in Southwestern Indiana." Newspaper Clipping, source and date unknown.

Worl, Gene. Round Barns of Indiana. Indiana Room, Indiana State Library, Indianapolis. 1967–69. Photocopy.

Yoder, M. S. "Building a Concrete Silo," *Farmer's Guide*, Dec. 16, 1911.

———. "A Concrete Barn." *Dakota Farmer*, Apr. 15, 1910.

———. "A Concrete Barn." *Indiana Farmer*, May 8, 1909.

———. "A Twelve Sided Cement Barn." *Farmer's Guide*, June 20, 1908.

———. "A Twelve Sided Cement Barn." *Farmer's Guide*, Aug. 23, 1908.

———. "Yoder's Cement Barn." *Hoard's Dairyman*, Jan. 8, 1909.

———. "Yoder's Concrete Barn." *Farmer's Guide*, Dec. 12, 1908.

———. "Yoder's Stable Plans." *Hoard's Dairyman*, Apr. 16, 1909.

Index